JESUS AND HIS
TEACHINGS

JESUS AND HIS TEACHINGS

Who Jesus is and what he taught as seen through
a careful study of the nature, trustworthiness,
and content of the Synoptic Gospels

FRED L. FISHER

BROADMAN PRESS
Nashville, Tennessee

Library of Congress Catalog Card Number: 74-189502
Dewey Decimal Classification: 232.95
Printed in the United States of America

PREFACE

Christian theology, especially New Testament theology, is primarily a theology about Jesus Christ. One could say (and some have said) that the truth or falsity of theology is not connected with Jesus of Nazareth. It is said that it is not necessary to ask about what Jesus thought of himself, what he taught, or what he expected his life to accomplish.

I would not want to rest my whole case for the truth of the gospel message on our ability to recover the words and intentions of Jesus, but it seems to me that New Testament theology *necessarily* rests upon the foundation of the life, teachings, and redemptive action of Jesus. At least, the writers of our Gospels thought so. Therefore, it is necessary to ask seriously about the Jesus of the Gospels, to inquire into the reliability of the gospel witness, and then to seek to understand the main elements in his teaching.

This book is an attempt to accomplish this purpose. It is an attempt to base conclusions upon results that will stand up against critical inquiry. To some it may seem that too much attention has been directed to critical investigation. The climate of our day demands this. The ultimate result, however, should be a better understanding both of Jesus and of our own existence in the world.

Notations in this book do not follow accepted form in every instance. At the first mention of a book, the usual bibliographical information is given. Thereafter, the author's last name with an abbreviated title of the book is used; the use of *op. cit.* has purposely been avoided in most cases.

Well-known works are usually referred to without giving full data. Most readers can recognize *The Interpreter's Bible, The Interpreter's Dictionary of the Bible,* and the *Theological Dictionary of the New Testament* (i.e., *TDNT*) without further identification.

Theological journals have usually been referred to by their common abbreviations. *NTS* stands for *New Testament Studies; JBL* stands for the *Journal of Biblical Literature; Int.* stands for *Interpretation.* Other abbreviations should be self-explanatory.

When it is not stated otherwise, the scriptural quotations come from the Revised Standard Version.

Quotations from foreign language books are usually paraphrased from my own translation. They are not usually put in quotations.

CONTENTS

PART II

THE TEACHINGS OF JESUS

CHAPTER I
THE JESUS OF THE GOSPELS

What are the features of the Jesus of our Gospels? They are so familiar that they need not be traced in detail. Yet, we must make sure that our conception of the picture of Jesus the Gospels presents is true to the Gospels. We will restrict our study to the Synoptic Gospels—Matthew, Mark, and Luke. This is not to say that John's picture is essentially different; it is actually much the same. Devout people in all ages have moved from one Gospel to the other without feeling any sense of strangeness in the Jesus they confront.

There is, however, a difference in the way in which the picture is presented. In John, the complete picture is present from the beginning. In the Synoptics, the picture unfolds. There is a sense of progression, often unnoticed by devout readers because they know the end of the story.

1. The Resurrection

"He has risen." This was the greeting of the young man to the tearful women by the empty tomb (Mark 16:6). The cry burst like a thunderclap on their ears; it filled their hearts with wonder. They hardly dared to believe it was true. That message turned the first frenzied Easter into a day of rejoicing; it dispelled the darkness and gloom created by the cross.

This is where we must begin our study of the Gospel portrait of Jesus; this is where the Gospel writers really began. Belief in the resurrection of Jesus is the foundation of Christianity. It gave impetus to the gospel message. This belief produced the books of our New Testament. It cast its radiance on the future, but it illuminated the past as well.[1] "No fact was more important for the primitive faith than the resurrection of Jesus."[2]

Whether we accept Willi Marxsen's suggestion that Mark was written backwards or not,[3] the implications of the statement are certainly correct. Everything in Mark, and the other Gospels also, was written from the post-resurrection viewpoint. The Gospel writers let the light of his resurrection shine back on the life of Jesus of Nazareth. It enabled them to see that life in its full meaning rather than as a collection of *brute facts*.

If one were writing a life of Jesus, he would naturally start with the beginning—his birth or entrance into public life. Our Gospels seem to do this. But this beginning misleads us. It makes us think that the Gospel writers were trying to write a life of Jesus. They were not. They were attempting to write gospels—testimonies to the meaning of the risen Christ for men of their own day. Not what Jesus *was* but what he *is* engrossed their minds. They saw the whole career of Jesus from the standpoint of the risen Christ. They recognized that the correct starting point in setting forth that career was his resurrection.[4]

If we want to understand the Gospels, we must begin where they began. The resurrection must be the beginning of the portrait of Jesus, not its end. Nor must we be concerned with the impossibility of finding a pattern in the accounts of the resurrection appearance. That first day was a frenzied day; it introduced a time of confusion and reorientation into the lives of the disciples. They were not concerned with what concerns us. They make no attempt to reconcile all the accounts

[1] John Reumann, *Jesus in the Church's Gospels* (London: S.P.C.K., 1970), p. 123.
[2] Maurice Goguel, *The Birth of Christianity* (New York: Macmillan, 1954), p. 58.
[3] *Introduction to the New Testament* (Oxford: Bail Blackwell, 1968), pp. 134-5.
[4] Floyd V. Filson, "The Focus of History," *Interpretation*, Jan. 1948, pp. 24-38.

of the appearances of Jesus. One fact, only one, was important—"He has risen."

Each Gospel has an account of the resurrection. Each handles his material in a unique way. Mark simply states that the women found the empty tomb, were told that Jesus had risen, and went away with fear (Mark 16:1-8). It is not certain that Mark ended here originally. It is certain that the verses which follow in our present texts were added by a later hand.[5] Perhaps Mark wrote more; this is surely a strange way to end a Gospel. If he wrote more, however, we do not know what it was.

Matthew repeats Mark's story in its essence (28:1-10) but adds other features. He alone tells of the bribing of the soldiers to say that the body of Jesus had been stolen by his disciples (28:11-15). If the fact of the empty tomb does not impress modern scholars, it certainly was important to the opponents of early Christianity. Matthew also tells of the Great Commission delivered to the eleven in Galilee (28:16-20).

Luke also repeats Mark's story of the empty tomb with some variations (24:1-12). He adds accounts of three appearances of Jesus which are not found in the other Gospels: to the two on the road to Emmaus (24:13-35); to the disciples in Jerusalem (24:36-49); and to the group at his ascension (24:50-53).

Each Gospel is different; the details are difficult, if not impossible, to harmonize.[6] Yet one thing is unmistakably clear. He is risen. To this fact each writer gives clear testimony.

They shared this belief in the fact of the resurrection with all Christians. John, Paul, Hebrews, and Peter give testimony to it as does the book of Acts. All scholars admit that early Christians believed in the resurrection of Jesus; this is an incontrovertible fact of history. These early believers saw in the resurrection the validation of the cross, the beginning of the Christian mission, and the basis for the enduing of the community with power for its task.

The resurrection is fact. In popular language, it is a historical fact since the appearances were to men who lived in this world. In technical language, it is a supra-historical fact. The appearances were only to believers and the resurrection cannot be verified by unbiased witnesses. We need not argue this distinction. His resurrection was far more

[5] This is one of the universally accepted results of textual criticism.
[6] Goguel, *op. cit.*, p. 58.

than a resuscitation. It was not a return to ordinary, earthly life only to be subject to death again. It was a resurrection. It was a lifting up of Jesus to a new plane of existence, power, and authority. It was his exaltation. To affirm the resurrection of Jesus, therefore, is not to make a historical statement; it is to make an affirmation of faith.[7]

It is necessary to remember that the Gospel writers were post-resurrection Christians who did not doubt the fact of the resurrection. They were not interested in reconstructing a life of Jesus, in presenting him as men had seen him during his earthly ministry.

They believed in a necessary and causal relation between Jesus of Nazareth and the risen Christ. They attempted to show that relationship by reporting (not inventing) incidents in the life of Jesus as seen in their full meaning in history. They were biased witnesses, *but they were witnesses.*

Many demand an unbiased witness. This is an impossible demand. There are none and never have been. A day-to-day chronicle, if one had been written, of Jesus' life would have reflected the attitude of the writer just as much as our Gospels. Imagine the difference between a chronicle written by Judas Iscariot, Caiaphas, or Pilate and one written by Peter, James, or John. Even so, a chronicle written by Peter, James, or John during Jesus' life would not have been as true to the meaning of that life as our Gospels are. The disciples did not understand the real meaning of Jesus' life until after the resurrection.

We do not ask for unbiased witnesses. We ask only for trustworthy tradition, tradition that pictures Jesus as he really was and interprets his meaning for us as it really is.[8] This we have. This tradition begins with the resurrection of Jesus. It is based on that fact. All Christian faith begins with the affirmation: "Christ is risen."

2. Jesus' Death on the Cross

Jesus died the death of a common criminal, no, an uncommon criminal, on a Roman cross. How could one who had died in such a way be the Messiah of God, the Savior of the world, the Lord of life? This was a question which the Christian mission had to answer. To proclaim such a one as Savior and Lord would be like trying to

[7] The relation between history and faith will be discussed later.
[8] The reliability of our gospels will be discussed at length in another connection.

convince people that a popular rabble-rouser who had been put to death in the gas chamber was really man's savior.

His death had to be explained. This is why the story of the cross takes up so much space in our Gospels. The resurrection needed only to be proclaimed; the cross demanded explanation. The Gospel writers believed that Jesus' death was the climactic act of God in redeeming man. In this, they agreed with the witness of the rest of the New Testament, a witness which is summarized in the words of Paul: "God was in Christ reconciling the world unto himself" (2 Cor. 5:19).

The passion story was probably the oldest connected narrative in the Jesus-tradition. It was constructed to clarify one of the oldest confessions of Christians: "Christ died for our sins in accordance with the scriptures" (1 Cor. 15:3). The Gospel writers were not concerned with the brute fact—*Christ died.* They were concerned to show that his death was *for our sins.* The passion narratives are constructed to show that Jesus' death was in the redemptive purpose of God, that he was not really a criminal, that his death resulted from an ungodly conspiracy, that it was voluntary, and that the way of the cross is the way of discipleship.

Where does the passion story begin? This is difficult to decide. His whole life was a journey to the cross. Perhaps the climax is reached in the conspiracy of the chief priests and scribes to deliver him to death (Mark 14:1-2 and parallels). The bargain of Judas to betray Jesus (Mark 14:1-11 and parallels) completes the story of this godless conspiracy. The reason for Peter's accusation at Pentecost is revealed by the narrative: "This Jesus, delivered up according to the definite plan and foreknowledge of God, you crucified and killed by the hands of lawless men" (Acts 2:23).

The anointing of Jesus by the woman is interpreted as an anointing beforehand of the body for its burial (Mark 14:3-9, esp. v. 8; cf. Matt. 26:5-13). The willingness of Jesus to die, if not expressed, is at least implied in the story.

The story of the Last Supper and the institution of the Lord's Supper follows (Mark 14:12-25; Matt. 26:17-29; Luke 22:7-20). The disciples prepare for the Jewish Passover in the upper room. While eating it with them, Jesus foretells his betrayal. His death is no surprise for him. He then institutes the Lord's Supper as a memorial to his accomplished redemption and as a prophecy of the future messianic banquet in the kingdom of God. The emphasis of the story is that the death of Jesus accomplished God's redemption and became the foundation of the Christian mission. It was a new beginning. The last words of Jesus begin with a prophecy of his betrayal (Luke 22:21-23) and continue with an interpretation of the way of discipleship in terms of humble service (Luke 22:24-30; cf. Mark 10:42-45; Matt. 20:25-28). Luke adds a riddle about the two swords which is designed to teach that the Christian mission is not one of force (Luke 22:35-38). The denial of Peter is foretold on the way to Gethsemane (Mark 14:26-31 and parallels).

Jesus' last climactic conflict with Satan takes place in Gethsemane (Mark 14:32-42; Matt. 26:36-46; Luke 22:40-46). In agonizing prayer Jesus prepares himself to face the cross. Naturally, he recoils from such a death, but he finds courage to endure it in order to accomplish God's will. His prayer, "if it be possible, let this cup pass from me" should be paraphrased: "if it be possible to save the world in any other way, let this cup pass from me." This paraphrase emphasizes correctly that the cross was essential to man's salvation. For this reason, Jesus was willing to endure it.

The story of the arrest of Jesus (Mark 14:43-52; Matt. 26:47-56; Luke 22:47-53) speaks of the stealth and wickedness of his enemies. A band of soldiers is furnished by the high priest for this task. They come, led by Judas who identifies Jesus with the kiss of shame. Each writer makes it clear that Jesus did not resist arrest; he had set his face toward the cross and his purpose does not waver now.

The stories of the trials of Jesus are somewhat confusing; they furnish a ready ground for scholarly controversy. The Gospels agree that there was a Jewish trial before the high court of the Jews—the Sanhedrin. Jesus was condemned as a messianic pretender. From the Jewish standpoint, he was a blasphemer. The Gospel writers see him as falsely condemned; to them he was the Messiah. In Mark's account, Jesus is made to confess under oath that he is the Messiah (Mark 14:61-62; cf. Matt. 26:63-64). The Jewish soldiers then mock him (Mark 14:64-65 and parallels). These stories emphasize the wickedness of the conspirators. Even though they are men who are sworn to uphold God's law, they act as God's enemies.

Each Gospel records a trial or trials before Pilate, the Roman governor of Palestine. Each, with considerable variation, makes it clear that Jesus had committed no crime against the Roman state. He was unjustly condemned to death (Mark 15:2-15; Matt. 27:11-26; Luke

23:2-5,17-25). Luke inserts a story of a trial before Herod (Luke 23:6-16). This may very well be a true story, but it does not alter the theological meaning of the trials. Jesus was no criminal; his death at Roman hands was an accomodation by a weak politician to Jewish demands.

Jesus is delivered to the Roman executioner and led forth to Golgotha where he is crucified between two criminals who await execution. The story of his death is told with great vividness by Mark (15:24-41) whose story is followed very closely by Matthew (27:33-56). Luke, however, tones the story down and adds significant details which stress the triumphant aspects of Jesus' suffering (23:33-49).

Each Gospel includes an account of the superscription over the cross: "The King of the Jews" (Mark 15:26; Matt. 27:37; Luke 23:38). This expressed the official reason for the death of Jesus. Officially, Jesus died because he was the king of the Jews, the rightful king, whom the Jews failed to recognize and acknowledge.

Each Gospel records a final cry of Jesus from the cross (Mark 15:37; Matt. 27:50; Luke 23:46). Luke alone records the words: "Father, into thy hands I commit my spirit!" The words show that Jesus died victoriously. He was neither a criminal nor a disappointed derelict.

You see, don't you, how the passion story is written as a mixture of brute facts and Christian interpretation? The purpose of the account is not to take one to the cross. It is rather to take one to the risen Christ who was crucified for our sins. The Gospel writers did not try to reconstruct the story; they wrote to demand faith in him who had died and risen again.

3. Moving Toward the Cross

Jesus' life on earth was a journey to the cross. Each Gospel writer constructs his account to emphasize this. We are not always aware of the destination as we follow him in his way, but when we come to the cross, we know that we have reached the intended destination of the narrative. Though it may not be entirely true that the Gospels are passion stories with long introductions, there is truth in that commonly made statement.

Two motifs are present in the accounts of Jesus' public ministry: (1) Jesus lived in the shadow of the cross and moved toward it voluntarily, (2) Jesus prepared his disciples for their future role in the post-resurrection world. Though the details given, the arrangement of the incidents, and the degree of clarity with which Jesus spoke of his coming death vary greatly, these two motifs are discernible in each Gospel.

(1) The Beginning—It will not be necessary to review the details of Jesus' ministry. We will summarize the highlights and seek to show how they fit into the Gospel portrait of Jesus.

  a. *John the Baptist* conducted a preliminary ministry; he was the forerunner of Jesus. Mark seems to identify the Baptist more closely with the gospel than Matthew and Luke (cf. Matt. 11:12-13; Luke 16:16). However, each Gospel writer sees in the ministry of John the fulfilment of Isaiah 40:3: "The voice of one crying in the wilderness: Prepare the way of the Lord, make his paths straight" (Mark 1:3; Matt. 3:3; Luke 3:4).[9] He came in the power and spirit of Elijah (Luke 1:17; cf. Mark 9:9-13; Matt. 17:9-13). He proclaimed the approach of the eschatological age, a function which prophecy had assigned to Elijah (cf. Mal. 4:5-6). He heralded the approach of the kingdom of God, called men to repentance, and baptized them as a sign that they had repented (Mark 1:4-5; Matt. 3:6). He denounced the Pharisees for wishing to be baptized without first showing by their lives that they had truly repented (Matt. 3:7-10).

His ministry was the thunderclap of God's voice in a barren land. The cities emptied themselves of their inhabitants to respond to his call (Matt. 3:5). Even tax collectors and soldiers sought to be included (Luke 3:12-14). He had the manner and sound of the prophet and the multitudes questioned whether he might indeed be the promised Messiah (Luke 3:15). John, however, refused to be exalted by them but pointed to another who was to come—his superior who would baptize with the Holy Spirit (Mark 1:7-8 and parallels).[10]

John is thus portrayed as the herald of God's eschatological action in redeeming man. His story is not told for its own sake, but to testify to the significance of the "greater one" who would come after him— Jesus of Nazareth. The Baptist was the connecting link between the old dispensation and the new.[11]

  b. *The baptism of Jesus* by John the Baptist marks the beginning of his public life in each of the Gospels (Luke strangely has John in prison before the event, cf. Luke 3:19). Three motifs are found

[9] Otto Betz, *What Do We Know About Jesus?* (London: SCM Press Ltd., 1968), pp. 28-31.
[10] For a good discussion of the relationship of Jesus and John see Joachim Jeremias, *New Testament Theology*, Vol. 1 (London: SCM Press Ltd., 1971), pp. 43-49.
[11] W. T. Conner, *The Faith of the New Testament* (Nashville: Broadman Press, 1940), p. 30.

in the baptismal stories (Mark 1:9-11; Matt. 3:13-17; Luke 3:21-22; cf. John 1:19-34).

One, Jesus came voluntarily to the baptism of John. The reason is not entirely clear. None of the Gospel writers imply that Jesus had to repent of sins. It seems most probable that he was answering God's call to take his place in the new movement. From the standpoint of the evangelists, Jesus, as God's Messiah, was identifying himself with sinful humanity in order to become its Savior. He had to become one with those to whom he sought to mediate the grace of God.

Two, Jesus received the Holy Spirit at his baptism. As he came up out of the water, the Spirit descended on him like a dove ("in bodily form," Luke) (Mark 1:10; Matt. 3:16; Luke 3:22). The Gospel writers saw the descent of the Spirit as the enduement of Jesus with power for his mission. Of course, this insight came to them in the light of the resurrection. At the time, his disciples knew nothing of it, or, if they did, they did not understand its meaning.

Three, a voice from heaven spoke to Jesus and said: "Thou art my beloved Son; with thee I am well pleased" (Mark 1:11; Luke 3:22; cf. Matt. 3:17 where the voice seems to address the crowd). The two parts of the message spoken are commonly identified with two diverse strands of Old Testament prophecy. "Thou art my beloved Son" comes from Psalm 2:7*a,* "the coronation formula of the Messianic king of Israel." [12] "With thee I am well pleased" reflects the words of Isaiah 42:1, "the ordination formula of Isaiah's Servant of the Lord." [13] The combination of these two strands of Old Testament prophecy—the exalted king and the lowly suffering servant—was absolutely unique. In these words, Jesus is portrayed as learning (perhaps for the first time) that his pathway to glory was the way of the cross. [14]

c. The temptation of Jesus follows his baptism immediately (Mark 1:12-13; cf. Matt. 4:1-11; Luke 4:1-13). Satan tempts Jesus to deviate from the pathway of suffering revealed to him at his baptism. Each of the three temptations recorded by Matthew and Luke have this purpose. He is tempted to deny his trust in God and use his power

[12] A. M. Hunter, *The Work and Words of Jesus* (London: SCM Press Ltd., 1950), p. 37.
[13] *Ibid.*
[14] C. F. D. Moule believes that the second part of the voice has been misinterpreted. He points to the lack of conformity with the language of Isaiah and to the fact that "well pleased" attaches itself to royalty more often than to the suffering servant in the Old Testament. *Lectures at Cambridge,* Lent Term, 1971. Jeremias (*Theology,* pp. 53-55) sees the whole quotation as coming from Isaiah. He believes the whole emphasis of the story lies on the descent of the Spirit. The voice only interprets this. I would think that the traditional interpretation as presented is correct.

to turn stones into bread. He is tempted to pander to the love of the Jews for a sign and throw himself from the Temple pinnacle. He is tempted to seek secular power to accomplish spiritual ends by bowing down before Satan who claims all the power of the world.[15] To each temptation, Jesus responds with an Old Testament quotation. The power of the Holy Spirit enables him to turn back the bid of Satan and set his face with steady resolve toward the cross. He maintains the integrity of his commitment to God; he wants to be God's Messiah, not Satan's.

(2) The First Stage of Jesus' Ministry.—The first stage of Jesus' ministry is bounded on one side by his temptations and on the other by the great confession at Caesarea-Philippi (Mark 1:14 to 8:26; Matt. 4:12 to 16:13; Luke 4:14 to 9:17).[16] The Synoptics seem to limit the public ministry to one year. John, by his mention of various Passovers would indicate, with more probability, a ministry of three years. For our purposes, we need not argue the case. We are concerned with the features of the ministry, with the kind of Jesus who emerges in our Gospels.

This stage of his ministry was public. It was conducted in the synagogues, beside the sea, on the roads, and in the village streets. Only rarely does Jesus withdraw from the crowds. It was primarily a ministry of preaching and teaching accompanied by the performance of various miracles (nineteen are recorded in this material in our Gospels). In this material, a number of the features of Jesus emerge.

a. *Jesus is the ideal man of God.* The true humanity of Jesus is everywhere assumed. He hungers and thirsts and grows weary as other men do. He is tempted to sin. He grows angry at times and is irritated with the slowness of his disciples to believe. He must pray for God's power as other men do. But his manhood is not that of the average man. It is manhood as God meant it to be, the manhood of one who loves God supremely and his fellowmen as himself. One might say that his humanity was *normal* humanity; it set the norm by which all other lives are to be judged. He insists that others pray for forgiveness; he never does. He tells others to repent; he never does. He advised others to seek salvation, but he never sought it for himself.

---

[15] Hunter, *op. cit.,* pp. 38-40. Jeremias (*Theology,* pp. 71-72) thinks the stories originally circulated as three independent versions of some ordeal of Jesus. He sees the theme of all three as being the same: "the emergence of Jesus as a political Messiah." I do not find his arguments convincing.
[16] This may be accepted as reasonable without insisting upon a strict chronological arrangement of the Gospel materials.

He emerges as one who is conscious of living a life that is perfectly pleasing to God.[17]

At the same time, there is no boasting about him. He is righteous without being self-righteous. He obeys God in all things but does not condemn the weak and sinful. Though the Gospel writers never explicitly present him as an example to be followed, the picture of the ideal man is there for all to see.

b. *Jesus is the eschatological prophet of God.* There is considerable difference of opinion about the category which best describes Jesus' work. Jeremias insists that he was more prophet than teacher.[18] Conner thinks of him primarily as a teacher.[19] Perhaps it is best to think of him as both.[20] There can be no doubt that the people thought of him as a prophet; there is a constant echo of this opinion in our Gospels (cf. Mark 6:15; 8:28 and parallels; cf. also Luke 7:16). Jesus himself never claims the title, nor did he reject it. He called the Baptist more than a prophet (Matt. 11:9); no doubt he felt the title was inadequate to describe his own ministry as well.[21]

Yet his ministry was sufficiently like that of the prophet to justify the title, no matter how inadequate it was. He came, as John had before him, proclaiming the approach of the kingdom of God and calling on men to repent (Matt. 4:17). He regarded his ministry as the fulfilment "of time" (Mark 1:15), of "scripture" (Luke 4:21), of "the law" (Matt. 5:17), and of "all righteousness" (Matt. 3:15). In all of his words, there is a sense of urgency, a feeling that the "end of time" has come. The authority with which he speaks reminds us of the voice of the prophets as well.

There is another sense in which Jesus filled the role of the prophet. He possessed the Spirit, or, better, was possessed by the Spirit. To the Jews, the Holy Spirit was preeminently the spirit of prophecy; one who possessed the spirit was a prophet.[22] Jesus repeatedly claimed that his power was the power of the Holy Spirit. By it he cast out demons (Luke 11:20; Matt. 12:28). He applied the words of Isaiah, "The Spirit of the Lord is upon me," to himself (Luke 4:18).

c. *Jesus is the teacher of righteousness.* He is often said to teach

[17] Conner, *Faith,* pp. 40-41.
[18] *Theology,* p. 77.
[19] *Faith,* pp. 50-53.
[20] G. Bornkamm, *Jesus of Nazareth* (New York: Harper and Row, 1960), pp. 56-57.
[21] C. K. Barrett, *The Holy Spirit and Gospel Tradition* (London: S.P.C.K., Paperback, 1966. First edition, 1947), p. 98.
[22] *Ibid.,* pp. 97-98.

and is often called teacher.[23] A considerable body of his teaching is preserved in our Gospels. The modern man would call it "ethical." Jesus would no doubt have called it "religious." The direction of his concern was conformity to the will of God, not to the customs of men. A large collection of this material is found in the Sermon on the Mount (Matt. 5–7; Luke 6:20-49). Another collection is preserved as a group of parables (cf. Mark 4:1-34; Matt. 13:1-52; Luke 8:4-18). Teachings about practical religious life permeate the record of his words.

As to the *manner* of his teaching, two things are said. He taught in parables, and he taught with authority. That Jesus taught in parables cannot be doubted. His parables constitute one of the oldest strands of tradition. It is commonly admitted that in them we come closer to the real Jesus than anywhere else in our Gospels. Most of the parables were kingdom parables, but some dealt with moral and religious attitudes.

"He taught them as one who had authority, and not as their scribes" (Matt. 7:29) echoes a number of such statements found in our Gospels (cf. Mark 1:22,27; Luke 4:32). This probably means that he taught directly without reference to the interpretations of the past. He spoke as one who knew what he was talking about.

The *reaction* to his teaching was mixed. The crowds loved him. They followed him gladly and hung on his every word with joy. The Jewish leaders, particularly the Pharisaic circles, refused to accept him. His teachings ran counter to their beliefs; his teachings constituted a slap in the face for all religious feelings of that time. They met him with incomprehension (Luke 15:29), dismay (Luke 15:2), abuse (Matt. 11:19), charges of blasphemy (Mark 2:7) and even sought to alienate his disciples from him (Mark 2:16).[24]

No one understood the true meaning of his teaching. The multitudes tried to fashion him after their own mold. The disciples failed to see the real depth of it. Even his friends came to think of him as mad (Mark 3:21). Yet his teaching lived on. Embedded in our Gospels, it constitutes one of the treasures of the ages. Jesus was preeminently a teacher.

d. *Jesus performed miracles but he was not a miracle worker.* His miracles were sometimes an embarrassing adjunct to his teaching.

[23] Conner, *Faith*, p. 40.
[24] Jeremias, *Theology*, p. 118.

He tried to keep them secret from the multitudes. Even the smallness of the number of miracles recorded shows how secondary miracle was to his ministry. There are scarcely more than thirty-seven miracles recorded in our Gospels (only nineteen as belonging to this period).[25]

But that he performed acts which were regarded as miracles by his contemporaries cannot be doubted. It is impossible to work back through the various strata of Gospel tradition and find anywhere a tradition of a nonmiraculous Jesus.[26] The Synoptic Gospels give evidence with remarkable unity that he did perform miracles.

The historian cannot deny his miracles and remain a historian. The historian seeks to discover a chain of cause-effect relations and make sense out of history. But the cause need not always be natural. Sometimes only a supernatural cause will explain a particular event. The scientist cannot deny the miracles and remain a scientist. Science has nothing to say about the matter. Natural science is concerned with repeatable, observable, and predictable phenomena of nature. No scientist has sufficient knowledge of the universe to rule out the possibility of miracle.

But why did Jesus work miracles? If he was not a miracle worker, if miracles were a mere adjunct to his teaching, if they embarrassed him with the multitudes seeking miracles, why did he work them? The biblical answer seems to be that miracles were meant to authenticate him as a messenger from God. Nicodemus understood them in this way (John 3:2) and sought knowledge from him as a teacher. Miracles, in the Bible, are limited to new departures in God's redemptive work. Moses and Joshua performed miracles to show that God was behind their giving of the law and the founding of the nation. Their successors did not. Elijah and Elisha performed miracles to show that God was behind the movement in Israel's history which is called the prophetic movement. Their successors did not. Jesus and his immediate disciples performed miracles to show that God was behind the founding of the Christian movement. Their successors did not. Thus, it would seem to be true that Jesus performed miracles to show that he was a messenger from God, that his teaching had the authority of God behind it.

e. *Jesus is the friend of outcasts.* One of the assured results of Gospel research is that Jesus' conduct shocked the Jews. He not only taught

[25] Reumann, *Jesus,* p. 205.
[26] Conner, *Faith,* p. 48.

in words but also by his actions. He kept company with the outcasts, the disenfranchised, the tax collectors and sinners. When his conduct was called into question (Luke 15:1-2), he defended it as reflecting the fatherly love of God. God is concerned about the lost; so, consequently, is Jesus. Yet there was never any suggestion that Jesus condoned sin. He kept company with sinners, but did not share their sin. He sought to bring them to forgiveness and a new life.

(3) The Turning Point in Jesus' Ministry.—Mark records a confession by the disciples at Caesarea-Philippi in which they acknowledged that Jesus was Messiah (Mark 8:27-33). Matthew expands the account (16:13-23); Luke abbreviates it (Luke 9:18-22). The basic ingredients of the story are: a question by Jesus concerning the popular opinions expressed about him (Mark 8:27); a reply by the disciples (v. 28), a question by Jesus confronting them with the necessity of personal decision (v. 29*a*); the reply of Peter (speaking for the group), "You are the Christ" (v. 29*b*). This is followed by a charge of secrecy (v. 30), the prediction of the cross (v. 31), an objection by Peter (v. 32), and a scathing denunciation of Peter as the spokesman of Satan (v. 33).[27]

There is no doubt that the Gospel writers thought of this event as the turning point, the great divide, in the ministry of Jesus. It represents a climax of the early ministry and a preparation for the continuing ministry. The accounts indicate that Jesus knew himself to be the Messiah but not according to the ordinary conception of messiahship. He was reluctant to accept the title and immediately pointed to "the Son of Man" as a better title for himself.

The reason becomes clear in the dialogue with Peter. Peter rejected the prophecy of the cross because it did not fit into his conception of messiahship. Jesus denounced his attitude as that of Satan. The concept of the Messiah had to be retailored to fit Jesus rather than Jesus fitting his ministry into a preconceived mold.

(4) The Second Stage of Jesus' Ministry.—Following the great confession, the ministry of Jesus is turned to the preparation of his disciples for their future role. Connected immediately with the confession is a saying about the meaning of discipleship (Mark 8:34 to 9:1 and parallels), the story of the transfiguration in which the confession is confirmed (Mark 9:2-8 and parallels), a saying about John the

---

[27] Matthew adds sayings about the Spirit's inspiration of Peter, the founding of the church, and the keys of the kingdom (16:17-19).

Baptist being Elijah (Mark 9:9-13; Matt. 17:9-13), and the story of the disciples' failure but Jesus' success in curing the epileptic boy (Mark 9:14-29 and parallels).

Mark and Matthew then concentrate their attention on sayings in which Jesus predicts his passion and teaches about the meaning of discipleship. Luke does also but in his own peculiar way. His travel story (Luke 9:51 to 18:14) is a literary device to point out that the way of the cross is the way of both Jesus and his disciples. Though some public teaching is contained in these sections and some miracles performed, the primary emphasis is not on the crowds but on the disciples.

(5) The Last Ministry in Jerusalem.—The last days in Jerusalem (Mark 11:1 to 13:37; Matt. 21:1 to 25:46; Luke 19:28 to 21:38) constitute a meaningful climax to Jesus' ministry. The events and teachings described explain why the Jewish leaders conspired to put him to death.

His entry into Jerusalem (Mark 11:1-10 and parallels) is a deliberate parabolic action in which he seeks to present himself to the Jews as their promised Messiah. There can be little doubt that he deliberately staged his entrance to recall the prophecy of Zechariah 9:9; at least, the Gospel accounts picture it in this way.

Two symbolic actions teach the rejection of Israel. One is private— the cursing of the fig tree (Mark 11:12-14,20-25 and parallels). The other is public—the cleansing of the Temple (Mark 11:15-19 and parallels). Both point in the same direction. God has rejected Judaism and is replacing it with the movement which Jesus came to inaugurate.

A series of dialogues with Jewish leaders is also recorded. They are designed to show the superficiality and shallowness of current Judaism. The leaders ask about his authority (Mark 11:27-33 and parallels) and are condemned of disregarding the authority of God. The parables of the two sons (Matt. 21:28-32), the wicked tenants (Mark 12:1-12 and parallels), and the marriage feast (Matt. 22:1-14; cf. Luke 14:16-24) point to God's rejection of the Jewish nation.

The Pharisees are condemned of hypocrisy in their question about paying tribute to Caesar (Mark 12:13-17 and parallels). The Sadducees with their trick question about the resurrection show themselves to be men who know "neither the scriptures nor the power of God" (Mark 12:18-27 and parallels). Finally Jesus puts his opponents to silence with his question about David's son and David's Lord (Mark

12:35-37). The Jewish understanding of Scripture was not able to reconcile the two quotations from the Old Testament. Only the messiahship of Jesus could.

4. The Origins of Jesus

Mark has nothing to say about the birth of Jesus. He did not consider it a part of the good news. Neither indeed did Matthew or Luke. The stories of Jesus' birth, infancy, and boyhood are told as preludes to the gospel rather than as an integral part of it. Even John's interest in the preexistence of Jesus is restricted to the prologue of his Gospel.

This is not to deny the factual foundation of the stories of the virgin birth. The mere fact of their appearance in the Gospels as sidelights to the good news rather than as part of it indicates that they are based on solid tradition. Why else would such unbelievable stories be told? They are meant, in the theological thrust of the Gospels, to show that the category of humanity was insufficient to explain the phenomenon which was Jesus. While he was truly human, his life can only be explained from the standpoint of perfect unity with God. This unity, expressed in our Gospels by the birth stories, is expressed theologically by the Christian doctrine of the incarnation.

5. The Resultant Picture of Jesus

This survey of the Gospel material, though necessarily brief, has revealed the clear outlines of a portrait of Jesus. The Gospels agree; in spite of diverse ways of presentation, the result is the same. The Jesus of history has become the Christ of faith. His earthly career is viewed from that perspective. Its real meaning *for faith* shines through the Gospel records.

The Gospels can be summarized in the words of Peter at Pentecost: "Jesus of Nazareth, a man attested to you by God with mighty works and wonders and signs which God did through him in your midst, as yourselves know—this Jesus, delivered up according to the . . . foreknowledge of God, you crucified and killed by the hands of lawless men. But God raised him up, having loosed the pangs of death, because it was not possible for him to be held by it. . . . This Jesus God raised up, and of that we all are witnesses. Being therefore exalted at the right hand of God, and having received from the Father the promise of the Holy Spirit, he has poured out this which you see and hear. . . . Let all the house of Israel therefore know assuredly that God has made him both Lord and Christ, this Jesus whom you crucified (Acts 2:22-24,32-33,36).

In the Gospels, Jesus is presented as the one through whom God has redeemed the world. He came from God. He lived a normal (not an average) human life, coming gradually to an awareness of his uniqueness and of his call to be God's Messiah. He performed miracles; he taught and preached great truths; he called on men to repent; he promised forgiveness of sins. He lived with a consciousness of immediacy in his relations with God and of urgency in his relations to the world.

He died for our sins, thus accomplishing salvation for all men. He arose from the dead. He commissioned his church for its ministry in the world. He is the continuing Lord of the churches and is to be worshiped as one who is truly God. The gospel to be preached is the good news of God's salvation centered in him. His present position as Lord was earned by his earthly life and ministry. There is a direct, causal connection between what *he is* and what *he once was*. To the Gospel writers, his career is not irrelevant. It is essential to the gospel message.

PART I
THE RELIABILITY
OF THE GOSPELS

Is this picture of Jesus a valid picture? Does it represent him as he really was? Or, is it the creative construction of the Christian communities? Is it necessary to authenticate this picture in order to have a New Testament theology? These and other questions are the most vexing and perplexing concerns of New Testament scholarship today.

I believe that the picture is a valid one, that the picture of Jesus contained in the Gospels is true to reality, and that the *substance* of his teaching is preserved in them.

It is necessary to establish this fact, however. It cannot simply be assumed. The questions raised by modern New Testament scholarship must be answered. At the same time outdated opinions about the Gospels must be corrected. We must accept those valid insights about the Gospels which scholarship has discovered. Thus this part of our discussion will have a twofold purpose: one, to discover the true nature of the Gospels, and two, to establish their essential reliability.

CHAPTER II
THE NATURE OF
THE GOSPELS

What kind of books are the Gospels? Are they historical, theological, or biographical? Or, are they all three at the same time? This is an important question. The Gospels alone preserve the picture of Jesus outlined in the last chapter. Our knowledge of him rests almost wholly upon the material preserved in them. It is not fair or legitimate to judge the Gospels as *pure history* if they are something else entirely. Nor is it valid to judge them as *pure theology* if they contain history. We must judge first of all to what degree they are history and to what degree they are theology. Only then can we apply the canons of judgment which are relevant and decide on the reliability of the Gospels. All too often Gospel criticism has applied the wrong canons to materials within the Gospels. We must avoid that.

For instance, if a soup spoon is judged by its ability to excavate mountains, the verdict that it is a poor tool indeed is assured. But if it be judged according to its intended purpose, eating soup, the verdict that it is a very good tool is assured. So it is with the Gospels.

If one judges them as if they were *mere history* or *mere biography* he will soon find that they measure up very poorly.

They abound in supernatural elements.[1] They do not trace the course of events to show the cause-effect relation between events. They do not depict clearly the developing personality of Jesus. We can only approximately infer the age of Jesus, the year he began his work and the duration of his ministry. We know nothing about his personal appearance. Was he tall or short, thin or stout, dark or fair, robust or delicate? The Gospels tell us nothing of this.[2] Little is said about his mannerisms. His private life is given only passing attention. Even the course of his life is impossible to trace with certainty.[3] Many gaps exist which either could not be filled in or did not interest the Gospel writers.

On the other hand, if we approach the Gospel material as if it were pure fabrication, that the stories contained in it are fictitious, we soon find ourselves contradicted.[4] Near the beginning of each of the Synoptics we find that Jesus was baptized by John the Baptist. This is no fictitious story; it proved embarrassing to early Christians. It is "history as it happened." [5]

As we shall see, the Gospels contain historical statements which must be judged in the light of their factual accuracy, but the Gospels are more than mere history. They interpret the facts of history as well. It is interpretation that makes mere history become significant history. Events of the past must be understood if they are to have meaning for the present.[6] These interpretations must not and cannot be judged by historical methods. They are affirmations of faith which must be accepted or rejected on the basis of faith.

1. The Gospels Are Primarily Theological Works

The Gospels were among the last books of the New Testament to be written. The latest reasonable date is A.D. 70-85; the more probable earliest date is A.D. 55-63. At any rate, most of Paul's letters were written earlier. Why is this so? At first Christians had no interest in writing gospels. They made no attempt to collect a record of the

[1] C. K. Barrett, *Jesus and the Gospel Tradition* (London: S.P.C.K., 1967), p. 4.
[2] F. W. Beare, *The Earliest Records of Jesus* (Nashville: Abingdon Press, 1962), p. 18.
[3] Vincent Taylor, *The Formation of Gospel Tradition* (London: Macmillan, 1953), p. 144.
[4] Barrett, *op. cit.,* p. 5.
[5] Ibid.
[6] Ernst Käsemann, *Essays on New Testament Themes* (London: SCM Press Ltd., 1964), p. 21.

things Jesus had said and done. Why should they? Much was still remembered by eyewitnesses in their midst. Their primary concern was with the living Lord. Their central interest was in proclaiming Christ and calling men to faith in him.

As the Christian movement continued and expanded, there came a desire to have the words and deeds of Jesus written down and interpreted in the light of his meaning for faith. Probably three factors contributed to this desire. (1) It became apparent that Jesus was not going to return immediately. (2) The gospel had spread to lands and people who had no knowledge or memory of the earthly Jesus. (3) There was a need to give a solid historical foundation to the proclamation of the gospel. It needed to be shown that God had worked something in history which was ultimately meaningful.

The last reason was the primary one. The impulse to write gospels did not come from the historical concerns, but from the realization that it was just in the life and deeds of Jesus that God had reconciled the world unto himself.[7] Reumann correctly points out that when we "listen in" on the story of the cross, we hear men talking about what is central in their faith.[8] This is true of all the Gospel material. Faith in the risen Christ cast its illumination *backward* on the deeds and words of Jesus. They were now seen in their true perspective. They could now be interpreted in their real meaning. In a sense, this post-resurrection movement was a *"rediscovery"* of what had been there in the teaching of Jesus himself.[9]

We need not be surprised that our Gospels are not bare records of history; as such they would have had no meaning. Perrin is wrong in saying that there was absolutely no effort to preserve a historical reminiscence of the earthly Jesus.[10] But this was not their main concern.

The very name which they were given—Gospels—means that they are witnesses to faith. They state their facts with the purpose of communicating the "good news" of God's mighty acts in Christ.[11] Our Gospels constitute a type of literature which has no counterpart. They sought to convey religious truth in the framework of historical

[7] Beare, *Records*, p. 19.
[8] *Jesus*, p. 49.
[9] C. F. D. Moule, *The Phenomenon of the New Testament* (London: SCM Press Ltd., 1967), p. 46.
[10] Norman Perrin, *Rediscovering the Teaching of Jesus* (New York: Harper & Row, c. 1967), pp. 15-16.
[11] Hugh Anderson, *Jesus* (Englewood Cliffs, N.J.: Prentice-Hall, Inc., 1967), pp. 6-7.

narration.[12] What Bornkamm says about the great confession at Caesarea-Philippi could well be said about the Gospels in their entirety.
They do not convey historical scenes, but are historical records of
a "higher order." [13]

*(1) What the Gospel writers had to say about their purpose in writing
shows the Gospels to be theological works.* Their statements show that
the Gospels were not written for purely biographical or historical
reasons—to preserve the memory of what Jesus said and did. They
were written for theological reasons—to show the meaning of Jesus
for their own day. The Gospel writers were not systematic theologians;
they were pastor theologians seeking to strengthen the faith of their
hearers.

a. *John* explicitly states his purpose in theological terms: "Now
Jesus did many other signs in the presence of his disciples, which
are not written in this book; but these are written that you may believe
that Jesus is the Christ, the Son of God, and that believing you may
have life in his name" (John 20:30-31).

Three things are expressed in these verses. *One,* John made a
selection of materials; not everything was recorded that he knew.
This, in itself, means that the Gospel bears the imprint of the interests
of the writer; it stresses what he considered most important. *Two,*
the writer had a theological purpose—to convince his readers that
Jesus of Nazareth was the Christ, the Messiah, and the Son of God.
Three, the writer had an evangelistic purpose—to lead men to life
through believing in Jesus.

b. *Luke* is scarcely less explicit in his statement of purpose. "Inas-
much as many have undertaken to compile a narrative of the things
which have been accomplished among us, just as they were delivered
to us by those who from the beginning were eyewitnesses and ministers
of the word, it seemed good to me also, having followed all things
closely for some time past, to write an orderly account for you, most
excellent Theophilus, that you may know the truth concerning the
things of which you have been informed" (Luke 1:1-4).

Three things are apparent from this statement. *One,* the Gospel
of Luke is an account of what God had accomplished among men.
Two, it is an "orderly account." This could mean either chronological
or theological order. The latter fits the material better. *Three,* it

---

[12] Ibid., p. 7.
[13] *Jesus,* p. 173.

proposes to prove the truth of what Theophilus had learned orally.

c. *Mark* does not state his purpose, but his introductory sentence implies a theological purpose. "The beginning of the gospel of Jesus Christ, the Son of God" (Mark 1:1). This statement reveals that this is to be a "gospel," not a "life" of Jesus Christ. Christ is to be presented as the "Son of God." Obviously, Mark's intention was to present material which would establish the truth of this statement.

d. *Matthew* neither begins his Gospel with a theological statement nor states his purpose. However, a study of the structure of the·Gospel reveals a theological intention.

(2) The second-century Christians viewed the Gospels as theological works in the form of historical narration. The headings which our Gospels have today were given, not by the authors, but by the community of the second century. The best way to write them is: "The Gospel: according to Matthew," etc. The emphasis lies on the fact that there is only one gospel. This gospel is told in various ways, i.e., "according to" the writer. Romans could just as aptly be called the gospel: according to Paul.

It is time we recaptured this original understanding of the nature of the Gospels. Only thus can we avoid expecting something from them which they do not have to offer. These headings, when taken seriously, mean that each writer seeks to set forth the meaning of God's act of redemption in Jesus Christ. No claim is made that the Gospels contain sufficient material for a biography of Jesus. No claim is made that they contain reminiscences of the apostles. Later, Christians tried to force this information from the Gospels; they sought to make the Gospels into historical documents. This misconception has had to be surrendered in the face of new studies in the past two centuries.

This surrender, to some devout people, has seemed to be the surrender of faith in Christ. They have struggled against it and branded those who accepted it as heretics. Actually, it is not a surrender of faith; it is a surrender of a false understanding of the Gospels.

The Gospels were constructed in much the same way in which a modern sermon on the meaning of Christ is constructed. The modern preacher, if he uses gospel material, now in written form, modifies it (perhaps unconsciously) in various ways. He seeks to make the Christian faith relevant to his own congregation.

One, *he selects* various parts of the gospel material with a common subject or thrust. In doing so, he pays little, if any, attention to the order of the events he recites. His order is dictated by the theological or dramatic interests. A sermon on Christian love may be based on the example of Jesus, for instance. Various passages from the Gospels that reveal the love and compassion of Jesus may be used.

Two, *he omits* what is unnecessary to his purpose. He is interested only in telling enough of the incidents selected to focus attention on his purpose.

Three, *he furnishes* the event or saying with a new introduction. He takes it out of its setting in the Gospels and places it in its setting in the sermon.

Four, *he applies* his material in terms of the needs of his audience. This application may or may not be related to the application of the same material in its original setting.

Five, *he may add* material for the sake of dramatic effect. Some preachers may; most preachers do.

What is the response of the audience to this method of handling gospel materials? If it is done skillfully, the response is usually entirely favorable. The parishioner goes home feeling that he has a new understanding of Jesus as well as a new understanding of his own life as a believer. The preacher is not a heretic. He is not a historian. He is not a biographer. He is an interpreter of the meaning of Jesus Christ for the life of his people.

What the modern preacher is for his day, the Gospel writers were for their day. They were interpreters of the meaning of Christ for their own audience. They were not historians, though they were not unconcerned with history. They were not biographers. They were not theologians (in the modern sense). They were preachers who had a practical purpose—the edification and inspiration of their readers. They were pastor-theologians.

They handled their material in much the same way a skilful preacher handles his. They selected from their sources what they desired to use. They arranged the material for dramatic effect. They omitted what was not relevant to their own situation. They furnished new introductions which set the material in the framework of their own thought. They interpreted the material to furnish an application to the needs of their audience, often doing this by translating it into new terminology. They *may* sometimes have amplified the material to make it more dramatic. Those of us who believe in the inspiration of the Scripture believe they did this under the leadership of the Holy Spirit. Others may deny this. But that they did it is scarcely open to question any longer.

(3) The fact that modern scholars have been able to find particular theological motifs in each of the Gospels points to the fact that theology rather than history shaped the work of the evangelists. Of course, there is no agreement yet about the theological purpose of each Gospel. There is agreement that each has a theological purpose.[14] Three things, in my opinion, have mitigated against consensus in this area. *One,* many scholars have been too atomistic; instead of looking at the material as a whole, they have concentrated on single units and tried to read a theology out of that. Single incidents, especially changes which each evangelist made in his material, may be guideposts, but we must remember that each Gospel came to its audience whole. It was read aloud to them. The total impression must be the ruling matter. *Two,* many scholars have been too sophisticated in their analysis. They have attempted to press all the material of the Gospels into a single mold. They have found theological meaning in matters where it is entirely unlikely to be. The reading aloud of the Gospels would leave room only for dominant themes to emerge. *Three,* stress has all too often been placed upon the differences in the gospels. Differences do exist and are important. But we must remember that the material which they have in common is quite as much a part of each Gospel as the differences are. Christ is the central figure in each Gospel.

a. *Mark* is the first Gospel to be written; Mark created the literary form of the "gospel." [15] He is interested in Jesus mainly as a man of action, a doer of mighty deeds.[16] Although he often records *that* Jesus taught, he seldom records *what* he taught. His vivid realism is striking. His use of the historic present, the Greek imperfect, the word "immediately," and diminutives help to give the story of Jesus its moving power.[17]

Christ is the center of Mark's theology; his portrait of Jesus is at

---

[14] cf. J. Rhode, *Rediscovering the Teachings of the Evangelists* (Philadelphia: Westminster, 1969), pp. 47-240 for a critical survey of efforts by scholars in the past two decades to identify the theology of each of the Synoptics.

[15] Eduard Schweizer, *Das Evangelium nach Markus* (Göttingen: Vandenhoeck & Ruprecht, 1967), p. 11.

[16] Beare, *Records,* p. 20.

[17] Barclay, *Gospels,* pp. 172-175.

the heart of his Gospel.[18] He presents Jesus as the promised Messiah but must deal with the problem of his lack of recognition during his lifetime. Dibelius has called Mark "a book of secret epiphanies" [19] and this characterization is difficult to improve upon.[20] Schweizer has pointed out that Mark sees the whole work of Jesus as the word of God to man, his good news. He is not presented as a teacher, nor a magician, nor as abstract expression of God's grace, nor merely as an example. We cannot take his words without taking him. We cannot honor his works without honoring him. We cannot imitate his life without surrendering to him.[21]

In a word, Mark's Gospel is a presentation of Christ as the living Lord. It was through him that the good news of God's redemptive act came into being. He is concerned that his readers follow Christ. His primary concern is not biography but theology.

b. *Matthew* is the most comprehensive, most Jewish, and most ecclesiastical of all the Gospels.[22] It is revised and enlarged edition of Mark.[23] It incorporates and abbreviates most of the narrative material of Mark. It adds a great store of the sayings of Jesus, covering the main themes of his teaching (about half of these sayings are shared with Luke). It contains material about Jesus' birth, his public ministry, his death, his resurrection, and his commission to the disciples.[24] Matthew exhibits a tendency to omit or explain any ambiguities found in Mark.[25]

Matthew arranged his material as a vehicle of teaching. The stamp of his personality is seen in the arrangement of the teaching material into five great discourses, each of which has its distinctive theme.[26] Each discourse is followed by a body of narrative material which illustrates a related theme. Because of this arrangement and the way it facilitates memory, Matthew has been the most popular Gospel in the life of the churches through the ages.

Twin motifs dominate Matthew—Christ and the church. His material

[18] Sherman Johnson, *Theology of the Gospels* (London: Duckworth, 1966), p. 22.
[19] Martin Dibelius, *From Tradition to Gospel* (New York: Scribner's, 1935), p. 230.
[20] Hans Conzelmann, *An Outline of the Theology of the New Testament* (New York: Harper & Row, 1969), p. 145.
[21] *Markus*, p. 11.
[22] Barclay, *Gospels*, pp. 210-223.
[23] H. D. A. Major, T. W. Manson, C. J. Wright, *The Mission and Message of Jesus* (London: Ivor Nicholson and Watson Ltd., 1937), p. 223.
[24] Filson, *Matthew*, pp. 2-3.
[25] Major, *op. cit.*, p. 224.
[26] Beare, *Records*, p. 20.

is arranged and sharpened to show that Jesus is the fulfilment of the Old Testament prophecy, the true Messiah of God. The theme of promise and fulfilment permeates the Gospel.[27]

Matthew uses three devices to emphasize this central theme. *One*, he uses a great number of Old Testament quotations, far more than any other Gospel, over sixty in number.[28] He introduces most of his quotations with some such formula as: "All this took place to fulfil what the Lord had spoken by the prophet" (cf. 1:22). In this way, Matthew seeks to show that the various events in the life of Jesus are a fulfilment of prophecy.

Two, he is careful to include the saying of Jesus that he did not come to destroy the law but to fill it full of meaning (Matt. 5:17). *Three*, more than any other Gospel, he includes material which stresses the royal descent of Jesus as the true son of David (1:1; 9:27; 12:23; 15:22; 20:30; 21:9,15).[29]

Matthew is the only Gospel writer who uses the word, *church* (16:18; 18:17). He believed that the church was the community of the end time. He has only a bare outline of church polity, but he includes much material which teaches that the church embodies the ideals of true Israel. His concept of the church is universalistic; it includes both Jews and Gentiles. Its mission is to the whole world (28:16-20).

Probably because controversy raged in his community, Matthew includes more material which condemns the practices of contemporary Judaism than do the other Gospels. He sees current Judaism as the corrupter of true religion. He included material to show that Jesus had not abrogated the law, that the heritage of the past was to be retained and valued. At the same time, he included material to show that the new far surpassed the old, that Christianity contained a better expression of true religion than Judaism. In all of this, Matthew was writing as a pastor-theologian to share with his audience the meaning of Christ and the church for his day.

c. *Luke* is the Gospel of universal salvation. There is more agreement about his theology than about that of the other Synoptists. The classic work on Luke's theology, too sophisticated by far, but nevertheless penetrating, is that of Hans Conzelmann.[30] He viewed Luke as writing

[27] Conzelmann, *Outline*, p. 145.
[28] F. C. Grant, "The Gospel of Matthew," *IDB* 3, p. 307.
[29] Barclay, *Gospels*, p. 227.
[30] *Theology of Luke* (New York: Harper, 1960), first published in German with the title, *Die Mitte Der Zeit*.

salvation history with the career of Jesus in the middle, the time of the Old Testament as preceding it, and the time of the churches' ministry following. Many have noted that Luke writes of the universality of salvation, that his is the universal Gospel.[31]

When comparing Luke with Matthew and Mark, several distinctive elements appear. Luke's is the most Greek of the Gospels, incorporating an elegance and beauty that is scarcely equalled in the New Testament.[32] Probably Luke was presenting the gospel to a new and educated group without ever forgetting the ordinary people.[33]

Luke has much special material including five miracle stories, thirteen parables, and some narrative material. Luke is more concerned about the poor, the outcast, the disreputable, and the sinners. But he alone records three instances when Jesus was invited to dine with Pharisees (7:36; 11:37; 14:1). He makes a larger place for women in his Gospel, relating seventeen incidents in which women play a central or equal role. He stresses prayer more than the other two. He includes songs of praise that other Gospels omit. Striking indeed is his concern with the work of the Holy Spirit. He mentions the work of the Holy Spirit seventeen times as compared with five times in Matthew and four times in Mark.

Luke often accomplishes his purpose by subtle alteration of material derived from Mark. For instance in the saying about cross bearing (cf. Mark 8:34), Luke adds "daily" (Luke 9:23). In the prophecy of the coming of the kingdom (cf. Mark 9:1), Luke omits the phrase, "come with power" (Luke 9:27). In these ways, and others, he changes the emphasis and stresses the "long haul" of history. Perrin is perhaps right in saying that Luke is concerned with the life of the community as it settles down for the "long haul of history."[34]

In the structure of the Gospel, two things are noteworthy. *First,* he transfers the rejection at Nazareth (Luke 4:14-30) to the beginning of Jesus' public ministry and focuses the attention entirely on Christ as God's agent of redemption in the first great section of his Gospel (4:14 to 9:50). *Second,* he constructs a journey narrative out of his special material picturing Jesus' journey to Jerusalem (9:51 to 19:27). On closer examination this journey appears to be a literary device

[31] Barclay, *Gospels,* p. 293 and Karl Rengstorf, *Das Evangelium nach Lukas* (Gottingen: Vandenhoeck & Ruprecht, 1958), p. 3.
[32] Barclay, *Gospels,* p. 276.
[33] *Ibid.*
[34] *Rediscovering,* p. 17.

to depict the way of the cross as the way of both Jesus and his followers. All of this adds up to the presentation of the one gospel of Jesus Christ with a special emphasis. The coming of Christ no longer looms in the offing. The church is faced with its continuing task. The gospel is for all men—outcast and respected, rich and poor, male and female. The way of Jesus has become the way of the Christian. Prayer, witnessing, and stewardship practiced daily are the prime requirements for believers. Whether we say that he was writing salvation history or emphasizing the universality of the gospel, we are saying much the same thing. Either statement expresses the theological concern of Luke equally well.

Thus we see that the gospels are primarily theological works. They must not be judged as if they were meant to be merely historical or merely biographical in nature.

2. The Gospels Are Also Historical Works

The fact that the Gospels are primarily theological must not blind us to the fact that they are also historical. They are theology written in the form of historical narration. Their theology is interwoven with statements of historical fact. "Christ died for our sins" (1 Cor. 15:3) is primarily a theological statement, meant to present the meaning of Christ's death for us. But it is also a historical statement. If Jesus did not really die, or if he died for his own crimes, the theology stands condemned.

What we have said must not lead us to feel that we are not concerned with establishing confidence in the historical statements of the Gospels. This is far from the truth. Let it be admitted, yes, insisted upon, that Christian faith is not merely a matter of historical certainty. Faith is a matter of surrender to the lordship of the living Christ. Therefore, we are not *only* or even *primarily* concerned with establishing the truth of historical facts—that Jesus lived, that he was crucified, that he was baptized by the Baptist, that he was a popular but misunderstood teacher. Our primary concern is with the divine dimension of history, its suprahistorical character—that Jesus was the incarnation of God, that he died for our sins, that he revealed the true God, and that he lives beyond the grave. No amount of historical evidence can prove this or compel faith in the living Christ.[35]

But, our faith cannot be a blind faith; such faith is no faith at

[35] Moule, *Phenomenon,* p. 78.

all. We do need to have some historical knowledge of Jesus before we can have faith in the living Christ. We need to know what manner of man he was, why he died, and what his credentials as Lord and God are.[36] The brute facts of history are important to faith. We ask now in what way they are important.

(1) Christian faith cannot be validated by the establishment of the historical facts alone. Bultmann has called the search for historical facts illegitimate because he sees it as an attempt to support faith by historical evidence. I would agree that it is illegitimate if that is the aim. Historical facts cannot validate faith. History cannot prove the truth of the gospel. "One cannot climb the ladder of historical facts to the world of faith." [37]

This is shown first of all by the fact that an encounter, even a continuous encounter, with the earthly Jesus did not always lead men to faith. There can be no doubt that Jesus was an extraordinary man. The people in general gave him a high place; they thought of him as a prophet, a rabbi, and a wonder worker. They ranked him with the top men of Israel. Even Herod thought he was John the Baptist raised to life again.

But there were notable exceptions. His friends thought him "mad" (Mark 3:21). The Pharisees and others saw him as a threat to all that was holy and right. They called him a "devil" and accused him of league with the prince of demons (Matt. 12:24). John the Baptist came to doubt his own identification of Jesus as the coming one (Matt. 11:2-3). Judas Iscariot was one of the twelve, yet he became a thief and a betrayer of Jesus. Matthew is right in pointing to the inspiration of the Holy Spirit as the source of Peter's confession of Jesus as the Messiah (Matt. 16:17).

The same is true today. If we had a talking movie of the life of Jesus from the beginning to the end, we would know more about the details of his actions and words than we can ever hope to know through the study of the Gospels. Yet, this knowledge alone would not compel faith.[38] Faith arises only when historical facts are wedded to spiritual insight. The inspiration of the Holy Spirit is as essential to our faith as it was to Peter's.

I would agree with Barth, Brunner, Bultmann, Tillich, Kähler, and

---

[36] *Ibid.*, p. 79.
[37] H. K. McArthur, *The Quest Through the Centuries* (Philadelphia: Fortress, 1966), p. 138.
[38] Moule, *Phenomenon*, p. 78.

Kierkegaard that faith cannot be based on historical inquiry. It is a falsification of both faith and historical study to base the former on the latter.[39] The virgin birth, if it were proved, could not of itself establish the doctrine of the incarnation.[40] The Christian simply cannot afford to be in a position where he must hold his breath for fear some new discovery, like that of the Dead Sea Scrolls, will destroy the basis for his faith.

(2) Nevertheless, confidence in the essential historical facts of the Gospels is essential to Christian faith. H. K. McArthur, in a penetrating article, points to three positions which are taken with reference to the relation between historical certainty and the gospel.[41]

One, there are those who, like Bultmann and Tillich, feel themselves immune from historical research. They deny that it is *theologically* important to know either precisely or generally what the true history of Jesus was. They admit that Christianity originated in a historical life, but they insist that it is encounter with the results of that life that is theologically important.

Two, there are those who believe that historical certainty is essential but impossible. They seem willing to accept the risk that historical research may disprove the historicity of the essential elements in the gospel tradition.

Three, there are those who believe that historical certainty is both essential and possible. They have diverse opinions about the way in which historical certainty is to be achieved. Some would insure it on the basis of historical study. Others would appeal to the inspiration of the Scriptures. Still others would rely on the authority of the church or upon their own experience of faith.

It seems to me that the third is the only possible position for the Christian. Historicity of the gospel tradition in its *essential elements* is both necessary and possible. This does not mean that the historical accuracy of the gospel must be demonstrated in *every detail* before faith is possible. It does mean that the *essential facts* must be established before faith can maintain itself intelligently.

There are three reasons for believing that confidence in the truth of essential historical facts is essential to Christian faith.

a. *Proof of the nonhistoricity of essential historical elements in the*

---

[39] V. A. Harvey, *The Historian and the Believer* (London: SCM, c. 1966).
[40] H. K. McArthur, *In Search of the Historical Jesus* (London: S.P.C.K., 1970), p. 19.
[41] "From the Historical Jesus to Christology," *Interpretation*, 23 (Apr. '69), pp. 190-206. Cf. McArthur, *Search*, for quotations from representative scholars.

gospel tradition would destroy the basis of faith. Faith cannot be based
on historical inquiry; history cannot validate faith. Yet, the negative
is also true. Faith could not survive if it were proved that Jesus did
not live, that he was not crucified, that he did not arise from the
grave, or that his teachings were quite different in content and spirit
than they are represented in the Gospels.[42]

If Jesus were proved to be a ruffian like Barabbas, a sycophant
like Pilate, a thief like Judas, or a worldling like Caiaphas, faith in
him would be impossible. This does not mean that the disproof of
some of the details of the gospel tradition would destroy faith. I am
willing to trust Luke's historical knowledge when he says that Quirinius
was governor of Syria when Jesus was born (Luke 2:2). But I do
not consider this detail essential to faith. If someone should prove
that it is not true, it would leave faith undisturbed, at least for me.
We are speaking of essential historical facts. If these were proved
false, faith would have to be forsaken.

b. *Lack of historical roots for the gospel would lead to non-Christian
docetism.* Docetism (the idea that the humanity of Jesus was only
apparent, not real) has been a danger to Christianity from the beginning. The tendency to docetism is present in every devout heart. It
is difficult to see how God could accomplish something ultimately
meaningful in a human life. The only guardian against a docetic
impulse is the solid rooting of our faith in history.

Bultmann has often been accused, and rightly, of fostering this
tendency by his insistence that faith is faith in the living Christ and
the earthly Jesus has no part in it. Many of his scholars, on the
contrary, have joined others in urging a renewed search for the historical Jesus and insisting that it is essential to Christian faith. "Otherwise
we shall be in danger of lapsing into 'kerygmatic-theological docetism.'"[43] Ernst Fuchs insists that the question of the immediate meaning
of Jesus is linked with the question of the historical Jesus. He denies
any interest in "exchanging this Jesus for some idea about him."[44]

c. *In insisting upon the truth of essential historical facts we follow
the Gospel writers themselves.* They obviously felt that there was a
causal, essential relation between the gospel they preached and the
life, teaching, conduct, death, and resurrection of Jesus of Nazareth.

[42] McArthur, *Search,* pp. 18-19.
[43] R. H. Fuller, *The New Testament in Current Study* (New York: Scribner's, c. 1962), p. 30.
[44] *Studies in the Historical Jesus* (London: SCM Press Ltd., 1964), p. 7.

It has often been noted that the very reason the Gospels were written was the concern of the early Christian community for rooting their faith in history.[45] Betz has pointed out that the community was fighting on two different fronts when the gospels were written. The Jews, accustomed to thinking of God acting in history, questioned the Christian faith in historical terms. On the other hand, there were those in whose thought historical fact evaporated and the humanity of Christ was denied.[46]

It was within this situation that the history of Jesus of Nazareth became an important bulwark of Christian faith and a guardian against heresy. Thus, the Gospels were written just because it was felt that the historical facts, the brute facts, were important and essential to faith.

This, I feel, must be the stand of the modern Christian. We must ground our faith in essential history. This is the only way that the view of Christ presented in our Gospels can be preserved. It is the only way that we can maintain an intelligent faith.

(3) How can we establish confidence in the historical facts? This is a question which will now concern us. Before beginning, let us notice the outlines of our task.

a. *We must first define what historical facts are essential.* One problem with conservative Christians has been that they have asked for too much. They want reassurance about all things historical. Often they have blurred the line between history and faith; they have tried to validate faith by history and history by faith. It should be apparent that not all historical facts mentioned in the New Testament are essential to faith. Faith could survive even if the visit of the Wise Men and the appearance of the angels to shepherds were proved false. It could not survive if the birth of Jesus were a fiction.

It would seem to me that we must speak with careful discrimination in this area. Upon what facts must I risk my faith? To me, these should be as few as possible. The existence of Jesus, the kind of person he was, his crucifixion, and his resurrection are certainly essential. Each scholar and believer must decide for himself what is essential and what is not essential to his faith. He must then seek to find evidence to establish his confidence in the truth of these essential historical facts.

---

[45] Käsemann, *Essays,* p. 25.
[46] Betz, *Know,* p. 13.

b. *We must define the kind of historical certainty which is required.* The historian approaches his task with the question: What degree of certainty is warranted by the evidence? [47] The man of faith approaches his task differently. He asks: what kind of historical certainty is essential to faith? Historical certainty may be a matter of literal fact or it may be a matter of *substantial trustworthiness,* i.e., trustworthiness as to the substance of what is reported. To illustrate, it does not matter to faith whether Jesus thought of himself in terms of being the Jewish Messiah. It does matter that the ascription of such self-understanding to him is in harmony with what he really thought of himself. In other words, it is the substance of his self-consciousness that is important not the actual title which he ascribed to himself. [48] Or further, it does not matter to faith whether Jesus actually, before his death, bade his disciples to take up their cross and follow him. It does matter that this demand is substantially the same as his demand was.

Thus the professional historian seeks one thing, the man of faith seeks another. The historian rejects all material which cannot be shown to be literally true to history. His treasure of validated historical facts will grow very small indeed. Even with this small treasure, the verdict must always remain in doubt.

The man of faith, however, seeks substantial reliability. He accepts all material which has not been proved false. His treasure of historical facts is much larger than the historian's. Further he has the right to be much more confident of their reliability.

c. *We must enter the arena of historical discussion and seek a solid historical foundation for asserting the truth of our Gospels.* The man of faith does not renounce the historian; he welcomes his work. Only by using it may the purposes of the man of faith be met.

It will not do to claim that the essential historical facts are true simply because the Scriptures are inspired. Our belief in the inspiration of Scripture is an affirmation of faith rather than a tool for historical research. Nor will it do to rely upon the living tradition of the church. Our findings may accord with that tradition; this may predispose us to grant veracity to the Gospels; it cannot give real certainty. Nor can we rely upon the evidence of Christian experience. Experience is subjective, too much so to have real value in dealing with historical

---

[47] Harvey, *Historian,* pp. 249-250.
[48] Cf. chapter 5 where this question is discussed at length.

facts. All of these may strengthen our confidence; none of them can substitute for historical conclusions.

Our procedure will be twofold. *One,* we will survey various movements in New Testament studies which have tended (whether purposely or not) to undermine confidence in the truth of the Gospels. None of these movements has actually destroyed the possibility of confidence in the essential historical facts. Some of them, contrary to the view of many, have tended to strengthen such confidence.

Two, we will then present evidence based upon historical study which confirms the historical reliability of our Gospels. The conclusions based on this evidence will then be supported by other relevant arguments. We hope to establish (or restore) confidence in the substantial reliability of our Gospels.[49]

[49] I admit that I am biased but deny that bias is an exclusive disease of the conservative scholar. All men are biased; they enter their studies with preconceived ideas. The only thing a scholar can do is to recognize his bias and seek to keep it under control. This I have done. The conclusions arrived at, in my opinion, are justified by the evidence.

CHAPTER III
CHALLENGES TO THE RELIABILITY OF THE GOSPELS

During the past two centuries, many movements in New Testament scholarship have caused ment to doubt the historical trustworthiness of the Gospels. While proponents of these studies, for the most part, have been sincere Christians, their work has tended to undermine confidence. These movements must now be sketched to show that they have fallen short of proving that the Gospels are not trustworthy accounts of the words and works of Jesus.

Generally speaking, these movements have attacked a misconception of the Gospels. As noted above, the Gospels were not intended to be primarily historical or biographical. They were first of all theological witnesses to the meaning of the living Christ. But this understanding of the nature of the Gospels was lost through the centuries. Justin Martyr (ca. 150) was the first to call the Gospels, "reminiscences or memoirs of the apostles." [1] Martyr's statement became the prevailing opinion of Christians until about 1800.

---

[1] A. Souter, *Text and Canon* (London: Duckworth, 1954), pp. 153-154.

This misconception is what has been under attack. We cannot accept all that has been said in these various movements, but we must recognize that they were a reaction against a misunderstanding of the Gospels.

1. The "Old" Quest for the Historical Jesus

The "old" quest may be said to have begun with the publication in 1835 of a *Life of Jesus* by David Strauss.[2] An important prelude to his work, however, was a fragment of H. S. Reimarus' dissertation on *The Aims of Jesus and His Disciples*.[3] This fragment challenged the prevailing opinion that the Gospels were biographical works. Reimarus believed that Jesus set out to become a political deliverer of the Jews and met with unexpected defeat and disaster. Consequently, Jesus died in an agony of disappointment. It was his disciples, who, after his death, resorted to the fiction of his resurrection and reinterpreted his ministry in terms of apocalyptic messianism.[4]

Strauss's work was more thoroughgoing than Reimarus'. He insisted on applying the canons of historical research to the Gospels and insisted that the infancy stories, the temptation accounts, the ascension, the baptism of Jesus, the mission of the seventy, most of the healing narratives, all nature miracles, the story of the transfiguration, and the resurrection, when critically examined, could not be regarded as historical accounts at all.[5] He felt that Christ's life was overlaid with legends created by the primitive Christians. He denied any historical worth to the fourth Gospel. Even the Synoptics contained different strata of legend and narrative.[6]

These two works laid the foundation of what is now called the "old" quest for the historical Jesus, i.e., the quest for what is historically verifiable about Jesus of Nazareth. The historical Jesus was what was left in the Gospels when everything supernatural had been eliminated by the historian.[7] Usually he was pictured as a gentle, Jewish rabbi who taught the universal fatherhood of God and the brotherhood of man.

[2] *The Life of Jesus Critically Examined,* trans. by George Eliot (London: Swan Sonnenschein & Co. 5th. ed., 1906).

[3] Harvey, *Historian,* p. 9.

[4] H. E. Dana, *New Testament Criticism* (Fort Worth, Texas: The World Company, 1924), p. 85.

[5] Harvey, *Historian,* p. 9.

[6] Dana, *Criticism,* p. 87.

[7] Harvey, *Historian,* p. 169.

The *basic presuppositions* of the "old" quest were three in number. *One*, it was supposed that the Gospels were largely the product of the early churches' imagination and theological explanation.[8] Thus, there was a fundamental discontinuity between the Jesus of history and the Christ of faith. *Two*, it was supposed that by using nineteenth-century methods of historical criticism, the hard core of historical fact could be located and Jesus, as he really was, would emerge.[9] *Three*, it was supposed that this "historical" Jesus, when found, would be a hero of faith and an example which would inspire men to live a noble life.[10]

The *close of the "old" quest* was heralded by the publication of two books. Martin Kähler "mortally wounded"[11] the movement by the publication of his book: *The So-called Historical Jesus and the Historic Biblical Christ* in 1862.[12] Kähler challenged the quest theologically by insisting that the Gospels are not dead records of the past, but living messages of the present. He was the first to make the distinction between *Historie* (an event of the past) and *Geschichte* (an event of the past which has present significance), a distinction still used by many scholars.

If Kähler mortally wounded the movement, Albert Schweitzer may be said to have written its "impressive scientific obituary."[13] His *The Quest of the Historical Jesus,* published in 1906,[14] challenged the validity of the quest on historical grounds. He showed that each scholar tended to create Jesus in his own image and ascribe to him his own thoughts. If this was possible, the so-called historical method was not scientific at all.

Thus the old quest died, discredited by its own excesses and the unscientific quality of the work of those who wrote in the name of science. But it left its mark on New Testament scholarship. Many came to feel that the Gospel records could no longer be relied upon

---

[8] W. Hordern, *Introduction,* Vol. I of *New Directions in Theology Today* (Philadelphia: Westminster Press, 1966), p. 57.

[9] *Ibid.*

[10] *Ibid.*

[11] C. E. Braaten, "Martin Kähler on the historic biblical Christ," *The Historical Jesus and the Kerygmatic Christ,* ed. by Braaten and R. A. Harrisville (New York: Abingdon Press, 1964), p. 79.

[12] Translated by Carl E. Braaten from the German: *Der Sogenannte Historische Jesus and Der Geschichtliche Biblisch Christus* (Philadelphia: Fortress, 1964).

[13] Braaten, *op. cit.,* p. 79.

[14] Trans. by W. Montgomery (London: Adam and Charles Black, 1910).

as historically true. Nothing could be known *for certain* about Jesus of Nazareth. Consequently, New Testament scholarship turned to the study of the Gospel records as a source for the history of early Christianity.

2. Form Criticism

Form criticism (German: *Formgeschichte,* i.e., the study of the history of forms) came to be applied to the study of the New Testament at the end of World War I (1919-1922). It was introduced by the almost simultaneous and independent publication of works by three scholars: Martin Dibelius, Rudolph Bultmann, and K. L. Schmidt. Dibelius' *From Tradition to the Gospel*[15] indicated the road to be pursued and gave a name to the new method.[16] Bultmann's *The History of the Synoptic Tradition* (1921) attempted to write the history of each individual paragraph of Gospel material and discover whether it had been altered or enlarged in the process of transmission.[17] Schmidt's *Der Rahman Der Geschichte Jesus* (1919) attacked the chronology of the Gospels by showing that the framework, i.e., the introductory statements of place and time, were artificially constructed.[18]

These three books opened an era of New Testament study which has continued to this day. The basic principles of form criticism have won widespread acceptance among scholars of all countries, theological persuasions, and ecclesiastical connections. Scholars have not agreed on the results of the study; they have agreed on the validity of the method. On the surface, form criticism seems to be a serious challenge to confidence in the reliability of the Gospels. This applies more to the radical conclusions of some form critics than it does to the method itself.

The *principles and presuppositions of form criticism* are variously described but may be listed as follows. *One,* it is assumed that an oral transmission of the gospel tradition preceded the writing of the Gospels.[19] The fact of such transmission can be, indeed, must be, accepted as true. But this does not necessarily imply distortion of the materials transmitted. The disciples of Jesus were Jews; they did

[15] Trans. by B. L. Woolf from *Die Formgeschichte Des Evangeliums.*
[16] Rohde, *Rediscovering,* p. 6.
[17] *Ibid.*
[18] *Ibid.*
[19] E. B. Redlich, *Form Criticism, Its Value and Limitations* (London: Duckworth, 1948), p. 10. H. Riesenfeld, *The Gospel Tradition* (Philadelphia: Fortress, 1970), p. 7. G. E. Ladd, *New Testament and Criticism* (Grand Rapids: Eerdmans, 1967), p. 148.

not depend on the written record; they remembered and transmitted their material orally. The *mishna*, the basic framework of the Jewish Talmud, was transmitted orally from the first century B.C. to the second century A.D. This includes an unbelievable amount of material.

Two, it is assumed that various units of the gospel tradition, with the exception of the passion story, circulated independently.[20] When the Gospels were written, the stories were joined together and furnished with an introductory framework of time and place. To a limited degree, the contention of K. L. Schmidt that the framework of the Gospels is artificial must be accepted as true. Of course, there is an overall progression in Mark's Gospel that is self-authenticating. Yet, it remains true that we cannot *with certainty* place any particular event in a particular place and time in the ministry of Jesus.

Three, it is assumed that the material in our Gospels can be classified by literary form. When each unit is separated from its place in the Gospel, it has a particular form. These forms have been classified in different ways. It seems that three classes can be accepted without question: sayings and parables of Jesus, pronouncement stories where the primary stress is on a word of Jesus, and miracle stories where the stress is on the miracle itself. Some critics claim to find legends, i.e., stories with the primary stress on some secondary character, in our Gospels. If these exist at all, they are very rare and fail to measure up *in form* to the true legend.

Four, it is assumed that the Christian communities created and preserved these various forms. We can readily see that pronouncement stories arose from the demands of preaching. Sayings and parables arose from the demands of instruction. Miracle stories arose from the demands of devotion. The forms reveal the context in which the stories were told. It does not reveal the source of the stories. They were not necessarily invented out of whole cloth. They could just as well represent reliable testimony to what really happened. The point is that the form in which the material was preserved was created by the needs of the communities in communicating and preserving their faith in Christ. The presentation of the material had to be intelligible. This would *not necessitate* change in content though it would influence the form.[21]

Five, it is assumed that the content of the Gospel material was

---

[20] Redlich, *Form Criticism*, p. 37.
[21] Barclay, *The First Three Gospels*, p. 113.

modified to meet the needs of the communities. This is where the debate becomes the hottest. Some critics would insist that the early churches created material out of whole cloth to meet its needs. Others would insist that only what Jesus really did and said was transmitted. Our position is that the material was *retold, interpreted, and translated* in order to focus its point on the questions which had arisen in the communities. Of course, it had to be translated from Aramaic into Greek when the Christian movement reached Greek lands (all of our Gospels were written in Greek). This, in itself, involves interpretation as well as transmission. More than this, the demands of Jesus, given in his *sitz-im-leben,* had to be interpreted to make the same demands in the new situation.

One example of this reinterpretation is found in Luke 14:26-27. In verse 26, the demand for radical obedience is made in terms of "hating" one's own family. This fits the situation in Jesus' own life time. It meant that a disciple must put the demands of Jesus above all earthly claims. In verse 27, the same demand is put in terms of "bearing the cross." This way of stating the demands of Jesus must have had its origin in the early Christian community. The cross had *no religious* meaning during the lifetime of Jesus. It took that meaning from his death. Therefore, it would be highly unlikely that Jesus would have used such a symbol. However, the use of the symbol preserves the *substance* of Jesus' demand. It is historically accurate in this sense. This is the kind of accuracy which we are concerned to maintain. (Note: This paragraph is an example of form criticism at work. It is apparent that one need not deny the reliability of the Gospels in order to work as a form critic.)

The danger to faith does not lie in form criticism; it lies in the misuse of the method. Some critics have insisted that a considerable portion of our Gospels consists of fabricated material. They have supposed that there was a creative generation in primitive Christianity, a generation which invented Jesus. This is simply incredible.[22] Wholesale fabrication and distortion of the tradition was made impossible by the existence of both Christian and anti-Christian eyewitnesses to the career of Jesus.[23]

Harvey K. McArthur has spoken of a "road block" to confidence in the historical accuracy of the Gospels constructed by the "more

[22] Riesenfeld, *Tradition,* p. 9.
[23] Ladd, *Criticism,* p. 163.

radical form critics." [24] The very fact that he speaks of one segment of form critics shows that form criticism *per se* does not erect the road block.

Form criticism can properly identify and classify the forms of Gospel material; it cannot pass judgment on the validity of the content of the material. So long as form critics limit themselves to their proper task, they are acting scientifically and one can speak of the conclusions of form criticism. However, when the form critic presumes to judge the truth of the material, he is no longer acting scientifically. His conclusions are not the conclusions of the form criticism. They are the conclusions of a self-styled form critic, usually arrived at to fit his own preconceived idea.

This is why McArthur must speak of the conclusions of radical form critics. In their hands, form criticism has stopped being a science. Could you imagine hearing that a certain chemical result was propounded by radical chemists while it was denied by conservative chemists? One might hear this said about a scientific hypothesis, but never concerning a scientific result. We must therefore regard the conclusions of radical form critics as to the authenticity and truth of Gospel material as a hypothesis. They are not facts based on the proper exercise of form criticism.

Actually form criticism has tended to give greater confidence in the historical accuracy of the Gospels. Its most sure result is that the tradition was a living tradition. It was handed down from Christians to Christians from the time of Jesus to the time of the written records. This fact tends to give us confidence in the *substantial* trustworthiness of our Gospels. I would agree that a broad social tradition is more reliable than dependence on one man's recollections. [25]

In summary, we may say: (1) *Form criticism is not a cuss word.* It is a respected and respectable method of study, the results of which are considered valid by a wide spectrum of New Testament scholarship. (2) *Form criticism is not an exact science.* The subjective enters greatly into the assessment of values so that the same criteria can lead to differing conclusions. (3) *Form criticism is not an unlimited science.* Not all New Testament problems can be solved by its use. It cannot assess the historical value of the content of the various units of gospel tradition.

[24] "From the Historical Jesus to Christology," *op. cit.,* p. 190.
[25] F. C. Grant, "Introduction to Mark," *Interpreter's Bible* (New York: Abingdon, 1951), V. 7, p. 632.

3. The Demythologizing Debate

The attempt to demythologize the New Testament had many antecedants, but it came into focus through the publication of two essays by Rudolf Bultmann (about 1941) and the reactions of critics to his essays.[26] Bultmann's avowed purpose was to restate the kerygma, i.e., the gospel message, in modern terms. He believed that the gospel message had been conditioned by the culture of the first century and must be reconstructed in terms that were acceptable and intelligible to the modern man.[27] He felt that the way in which the gospel message is usually presented offended modern man with its mythological framework and prevented him from hearing the message itself.

The debate, most heated during the 40's, might have been carried on with more profit and less heat if Bultmann had chosen a word other than *myth* with which to express his thoughts. Many think of myth as pure fabrication. Bultmann defined it as speaking of the "unobservable" realities in terms of "observable phenomena," of the divine in human terms, of the other worldly realities in this worldly terms.[28] If one can remember this definition, myth is not an objectionable word to faith. It is simply saying that religious language is symbolic language. Bultmann, however, is not always consistent in his use of the term and sometimes seems to imply that the "myth" is entirely false.

Again, Bultmann's contribution might have been greater if he had been more careful in his interpretation of the New Testament. He seems to have accepted the position of German fundamentalism as the norm of what the New Testament teaches. For instance, he suggests that the New Testament teaches that all who belong to the church, are baptized, and observe the Eucharist are certain of salvation unless they forfeit it by unworthy behavior.[29] In my opinion, the New Testament teaches nothing of the sort. I would react against such a statement as strongly as Bultmann, but I would not consider it a myth contained in the New Testament. It is a misrepresentation of New Testament thought.

Bultmann begins his exposition of the "mythical view of the world and the mythical event of redemption" with the statement that the

---

[26] *Kerygma and Myth,* ed. by H. W. Bartsch (London: S.P.C.K., 1953), contains the two essays, criticisms by five critics, and Bultmann's replies to his critics.
[27] Harvey, *Historian,* p. 28.
[28] Bartsch, pp. 10, 47.
[29] Bartsch, *op. cit.,* p. 2.

world "is viewed as a three-storied structure." In the center is the earth; above is heaven; beneath is the underworld.[30] No doubt this is true. This was the cosmology of the day and the New Testament writers shared it with the world.

However, the New Testament never makes this view an essential part of the gospel message. Devout people of today have no difficulty in ignoring this element in the New Testament and focusing their attention on the essential message of redemption. As a "whipping horse" this prescientific view of the world may be meaningful; as a reflection of New Testament thought, it is meaningless. As a matter of fact, modern man has never quite shaken loose from this sort of language; at least he has found no substitute. The New Testament should no more be condemned for its use than the modern newspaper which faithfully reports the time for the sun to rise and set.

More serious is Bultmann's interpretation of what the New Testament teaches about man's life on earth. He thinks the New Testament pictures the earth as the battleground of supernatural forces with man as a pawn in their warfare. Man is subject to demon possession or divine inspiration. His life is not determined by his own choices but by the forces that rule him. Both the course of nature and the course of history are controlled by supernatural powers and miracles are not rare.[31]

This, to me, is a parody of New Testament teachings. True, supernatural forces operated on earth and man was influenced by them. But this, in no way, absolved man of his own responsibility. His choices were what opened the way for supernatural powers to come into his life. It may well be that the New Testament view of supernatural powers operating within the world is more true than Bultmann's view that they are shut out of the world.

Even more serious is Bultmann's attack on the essential elements of the New Testament message. He sketches this in terms very like Dodd's which must be accepted as true to the New Testament.[32] The points are: (1) The last time has now come; (2) God sent his son, a preexistent, divine being to earth as man; (3) He died and thus made atonement for sin; (4) His resurrection marked the beginning of the cosmic catastrophe; (5) Death was abolished and demonic

[30] *Ibid.*, p. 1.
[31] *Ibid.*, pp. 1, 2.
[32] C. H. Dodd, *The Apostolic Preaching and Its Development* (London: Hodder and Stoughten, 1936), pp. 38-45.

powers were deprived of their power; (6) Christ is now exalted and made Lord and King; (7) He will return on the clouds of heaven to complete his work; (8) Sin, suffering and death will be abolished; (9) Christians already enjoy the first instalment of salvation through the work of the Holy Spirit; and, (10) The Spirit witnesses to the reality of their salvation and final resurrection.[33]

Bultmann believes that the idea of a return of Christ and the end of the world is "mythical eschatology," pointing out that it never took place.[34] He objects to the New Testament doctrine of atonement on the basis of its unintelligibility.[35] He finds belief in the resurrection impossible.[36] In a word, he rejects the whole construct of redemption as set forth in the New Testament. He regards it as outmoded and senseless to the mind of the modern man. He insists that the whole message must be demythologized and restated if it is to make sense.

Against such views, Bultmann appeals to the findings of modern science. He finds it incredible that a man could use electric lights and radio and at the same time believe in a world of spirits and miracles.[37] But his idea of science is located in the nineteenth century not the twentieth. Science once thought of the world as a closed system run by unchanging laws of nature. Modern science is much more modest in its claims. So much is unknown that natural law is now seen as a convenient summary of the present state of our ignorance concerning the universe.

Regarding the presence and influence of supernatural forces, including God, science has never had and does not now have any basis to make a pronouncement. To say that natural science has made belief in the world view of the New Testament impossible and senseless is inaccurate (if we wish to be charitable). Natural science deals with observable phenomena. Events of nature may be observed, but the forces that cause them must be the subject of theological and philosophical discussion.

The second objection which Bultmann raises is the so-called self-understanding of the modern man.[38] Modern man, Bultmann thinks, has a sense of responsibility for his choices and actions which makes

[33] Bartsch, *op. cit.*, p. 2.
[34] *Ibid.*, p. 5.
[35] *Ibid.*, p. 7.
[36] *Ibid.*, p. 8.
[37] *Ibid.*, p. 5.
[38] *Ibid.*, p. 6.

it impossible to believe in the "interference" of spiritual forces in his life. *Some* modern men may feel this way; it would be difficult to persuade a penologist or a public-school teacher that all do. It is very difficult to construct a modern man and say anything definite about his feelings, fears, doubts, and hopes. Even if one could, what man feels can never become the criterion of truth. In my opinion, Bultmann's reliance on this argument is without any real basis.

Thus we see that the two bases of Bultmann's rejection of the world view of the New Testament will not bear the weight of his contentions. We are not forced to deny that this world is the arena of conflict between good and evil forces, and that man, though ultimately responsible for his own choices, is subject to outside influence.

This is not to say that Bultmann has not made a meaningful contribution to New Testament study through his efforts to demythologize the New Testament. He has. Perhaps the most important contribution is his insistence that the gospel message must be restated in every generation. It is true that the way the message is preached in one generation and time is not necessarily relevant to another generation or time. The New Testament itself gives evidence of this. In stating the conditions of salvation, Jesus usually described them by saying that men must repent, Paul by saying that man must have faith, John by saying that men must believe. In pointing out the meaning of salvation, Jesus usually spoke of the kingdom of God, Paul of justification, and John of eternal life. There can be no doubt that they meant essentially the same thing by their expressions, but the circumstances of their times dictated their language.

But a restatement of the gospel must be a restatement of the *gospel,* not a distortion. When we consider Bultmann's restatement, we find a strange mixture of excellence and misinterpretation. He has shown real insight in characterizing the life of man in sin and in faith. He views life in sin as life after the flesh, life centered in visible, tangible reality.[39] He views life in faith as life centered in intangible, invisible reality.[40] One is authentic life; the other is inauthentic. With such a view, I would have no quarrel so long as these terms are not considered to exhaust the meaning of life in sin and life in faith.

At another point, Bultmann has completely distorted the gospel message. He views faith as faith in Christ which is further described

[39] *Ibid.,* p. 18.
[40] *Ibid.,* p. 19.

as faith in the love of God.[41] Faith instead of being surrender of self to the living Lord, is living life in the same way that Christ lived his. I think Bultmann loses his way here. He departs from the New Testament *message*, not just its language. Faith in Christ is personal surrender to the lordship of Christ in one's life. This surrender does lead to the true, authentic human life because it brings *me* into a right relation with *God.*

Bultmann has not succeeded in his effort to restate the New Testament kerygma in terms acceptable to modern man. He may have a message which modern man will accept, but it is not the gospel of Jesus Christ. It is a new gospel which is no gospel at all.

Another contribution of the work of Bultmann is his insistence that the gospel calls for *decision now.* This is not a new emphasis, nor is it exclusively Bultmann's. Yet, he has stated it in such ways and circumstances that it has reached the ears of a vast audience. Hearing the gospel is not an exercise in mental gymnastics. It is a life and death matter, for *me, now.* When I hear the gospel, I am confronted by the living God. I must react. I must respond. I am free. I may reject, but I cannot ignore, the call of God.

In conclusion, we must say that Bultmann's challenge to the historical trustworthiness of the Gospels has failed. In spite of his valuable contributions and penetrating insights, his main contentions have been based on inadequate evidence. The possibility that the New Testament is right still remains. Of course, possibility is not enough; we need a stronger certainty than that. But possibility must be established before it becomes profitable to investigate stronger and more positive evidence which speaks for the reliability of the Gospels.

4. The "New" Quest for the Historical Jesus

The modern quest which still occupies the minds of many New Testament scholars was instituted by Ernst Käsemann.[42] He delivered an essay to a reunion of Marburg old students in 1953 entitled, "The Problem of the Historical Jesus." [43] This was the kickoff of the movement which has been a burning issue in New Testament scholarship since that time. Bultmann had denied the necessity for or the legiti-

---

[41] *Ibid.,* p. 19.

[42] Harvey, *Historian,* p. 13 and James Robinson, *A New Quest of the Historical Jesus* (London: SCM Press, 1959), p. 12.

[43] This essay is contained in his collection of *Essays on New Testament Themes,* pp. 15-47.

macy of any inquiry into the details of the life of Jesus. He insisted that only the fact of Jesus and his death were essential to faith. Even after the new quest began, Bultmann maintained his position and refused to associate with it.[44]

Käsemann insisted that an inquiry into the life of Jesus was both essential and possible. It was essential if Christianity were to be preserved from the danger of "docetism" and saved from degenerating into "moralism and mysticism."[45] He pointed to the fact that the Gospels had been written in spite of the early Christian absorption in the exalted Lord. The early Christians had insisted on the identity of the risen Lord and the earthly Jesus.[46] They had felt it necessary to ground their faith in history. Käsemann believed that the grounding of faith in history *was* and *is* essential to Christian faith.

The new quest is not only essential to faith, it is also possible, affirmed Käsemann. He admitted the impossibility of recovering sufficient material to write a full biography of Jesus, but he insisted, there are pieces of Synoptic material which the historian, if he is to deserve the name, must acknowledge as authentic and genuine.[47] These are sufficient to indicate "certain characteristic traits in his preaching."[48] It was on these traits that early Christians built their message, and on them we must build our own.[49]

Käsemann's essay found a ready response among New Testament scholars; it started a movement which has been vital and dynamic since then. There is hardly a scholar who has not at least "dabbled" in the new quest. Many have devoted their full time to it; essays and books on the subject abound.[50]

The purpose of the "new" is quite different from the purpose of the "old" quest. Whereas the "old" sought to drive a wedge between the earthly Jesus and the theology of the churches, the "new" seeks to show a real and causal relation between them. It seeks to show a continuity between the Jesus of history and the Christ of faith, between the proclaimer and the proclaimed, between the earthly and

---

[44] A. J. B. Higgins, *The Tradition About Jesus* (Edinburgh: Oliver and Boyd, 1969), p. 1.
[45] *Essays,* p. 46.
[46] *Ibid.*
[47] *Ibid.,* p. 47.
[48] *Ibid., p.* 46.
[49] *Ibid.*
[50] Among the scholars who have contributed greatly to the new quest are: Günther Bornkamm, Ernst Fuchs, Gerhard Ebeling, Joachim Jeremias, Eduard Schweizer, Norman Perrin, R. H. Fuller, James Robinson, J. A. T. Robinson, and a host of others.

the heavenly Lord.[51] In this respect, the new quest has taken its stand squarely in line with the New Testament. This is why the most conservative scholars have found it possible to enter into the quest, at least, to the point of seeking to accomplish its primary purpose.

It is at the point of methodology that the new quest must be criticized. In the first place, the quest has tended to depend entirely and sometimes naively on form criticism as the one method of research.[52] While form criticism is a respected and respectable tool of research, it has very definite limits and these limits should be recognized. As a method of judging the authenticity of the *contents* of a unit of tradition, form criticism is irrelevant.

In the second place, the criteria of judgment used to distinguish authentic[53] and unauthentic material are both unreal and inadequate. The primary criterion is that of dissimilarity.[54] This means that a saying is considered authentic if it is dissimilar to and shows no influence from either "ancient Judaism" or the "early Church." Only that which is unique in the sayings of Jesus is recognized as authentic. Perrin claims that we can recover what is characteristic in this way, but that claim is open to doubt.[55] Hooker points out that it is only the unique, not necessarily the characteristic, elements in the teachings of Jesus which are isolated in this way.[56] Jeremias calls it a one-sided principle which allows all material which Jesus took up from Judaism and all material which the early Christians took up from him to slip through the net.[57]

Jesus was certainly original and creative, but he did not disassociate himself from his people. Nor did the movement founded on his ministry disassociate itself from him. Thus, it would be expected that many of the characteristic teachings of Jesus would also be found in Judaism as well as being embedded in early Christianity. As is true of every great man, the originality of Jesus would consist, in part at least, in his ability to distil and clarify the heritage of his own people. Thus, many of his sayings which show a strong affinity to Judaism should still be authentic sayings. Likewise, the mark of

[51] Harvey, *Historian*, p. 13.
[52] Betz, *Know*, p. 19.
[53] A saying in the actual words of Jesus or an unvarnished account of an event.
[54] Perrin, *Rediscovering*, p. 39. Perrin's discussion of criteria in this chapter is superior to most discussions of the matter.
[55] *Ibid.*
[56] M. D. Hooker, *The Son of Man in Mark* (London: SPCK, 1967), pp. 6, 7.
[57] Jeremias, *Theology*, p. 2.

true greatness in a man is that his statements are taken up and used by his successors. Thus much material which reflects the life and thought of the Christian community may well be authentic material. For example, Abraham Lincoln's Gettysburg Address, if it were stripped of all material which *might* have arisen from prior American life and of all material which *has* subsequently become basic in American life, would be practically denuded. Since we have the address in written form, we need not go to such lengths. However, this illustrates the lack of realism in the criterion of dissimilarity.

Another criterion which Perrin lists is that of multiple attestation.[58] This means that material which is found in all, or most of the sources which the Synoptic writers used can be accepted as authentic. Perrin thinks this is particularly valid in determining authentic motifs of the ministry of Jesus such as his concern for tax collectors and sinners. This criterion may be accepted as valid. It certainly increases our confidence in a report of a saying or action of Jesus if we find it in all the sources of gospel tradition. Yet, it need not follow that every saying which does not have multiple attestation is inauthentic.

Another criterion which Perrin espouses is that of coherence. This means that material which conforms in substance to that which is established as authentic by the principle of dissimilarity can be accepted as authentic.[59] This is a valid principle and one which we shall use in our next chapters. We can take it as assumed that Jesus was coherent, that there was an underlying unity in his teaching.

Perrin closes his chapter on methodology by urging that a consensus of opinion be sought in applying these criteria.[60] This is certainly desirable, but it seems almost impossible. Perrin at times seems to think that if he and Bultmann agree, a consensus has been reached. If all shades of theological opinion are consulted, if scholars of all types are included, consensus is practically impossible. This, perhaps more than anything else, shows the limitations of the methodology being used.

The new quest has not been totally successful even in achieving its goals. It has failed to reach a consensus of opinion on the great body of tradition found in the Synoptic Gospels. Scholars of equal standing and ability can and do reach different conclusions from the

[58] Perrin, *Rediscovering,* pp. 45-46.
[59] *Ibid.,* p. 43.
[60] *Ibid.,* p. 53.

same data. This indicates that it is not the data but the subjective presuppositions of the scholars which dictates the conclusions.

But the new quest has not been without its contributions to New Testament study. For one thing, it has reminded us that *Christian faith must be grounded in history*. No matter how much may be said in favor of *existential* interpretation, it remains true that the roots of Christianity are in the history of a man who lived at a particular time and place in history and accomplished the redemption of the world through his death on the cross.

For another thing, radical criticism of the Gospel material has resulted in *the validation of some elements in the material*. Some of the material has been shown to be completely authentic. Though much of the material which has been rejected may yet prove to be authentic, we can now accept some material as authentic and beyond question.

By comparing this small treasure with other material and using the principle of coherence, we can reach virtual certainty concerning a considerable portion of gospel tradition. From this, we can press on to a recognition of the *substantial* truth, i.e., truth in substance, of the gospel records. They may not be composed entirely of authentic material, i.e., material which reflects the very words of Jesus. They are composed of true material, i.e., material which is true to what Jesus really was, taught, and did. By this method of comparison [61] we reach confidence in the accuracy of the picture of Jesus which lies at the foundation of the Christian faith. The burden of proof shifts. Now, it is he who would deny the truth of a unit of gospel tradition that must prove his point.

5. Redaction Criticism

Redaction criticism (Ger.: *redaktionsigeschichte*) is a study of the editorial revisions in the Gospels. It seeks to determine the extent to which the Gospel writers have imprinted their own theology on the materials in the process of writing the Gospels. It stands as a challenge to confidence in the historical trustworthiness of the Gospels in that it assumes further modification and change in the tradition at the hands of the Gospel writers. As we shall see, this challenge is more apparent than real.

Redaction criticism received its impetus from the work of three scholars—G. Bornkamm, H. Conzelmann, and Willi Marxsen—

[61] See the next two chapters.

immediately following the Second World War.[62] Bornkamm's two essays: "The Stilling of the Storm in Matthew" (1948) and "End-expectation and the Church in Matthew" (1954) dealt with the theological motifs of Matthew.[63] Hans Conzelmann's book on *The Theology of Luke* was first published in German in 1954.[64] Marxsen's book on Mark, *Mark the Evangelist,* was first published in German in 1956.[65] The publication of these books placed redaction criticism in the center of the stage in New Testament studies and led to the publication of a great number of essays and books on the subject.[66]

The aim of redaction criticism is to restore the Gospel writers to their rightful place as authors and theologians. In a real sense, redaction criticism is a reaction to one excess of form criticism.[67] Form critics had described the Gospel writers as "scissors and paste men" who merely collected and strung material together. The fact that each Gospel was a unity which demanded investigation was largely ignored.[68] Redaction critics have maintained, on the contrary, that each Gospel writer was a theologian, and that, though limited by his material, each had a theological purpose in writing.[69]

One cannot really speak of a methodology of redaction criticism. The study is still young and there is no consensus as to the proper methods to be used. It is possible, however, to outline in a general way the steps that scholars have taken in pursuing this study.

First, each Gospel must be looked at *as a whole* to discover its purpose. It must be assumed that each Gospel writer attempted to give a distinct witness to Jesus Christ. The content of that witness is revealed by his selection, arrangement, and modification of his materials. Many critics have ignored this first step in redaction criticism and concentrated too completely on individual unity of each Gospel.

Second, the contributions of the Gospel writer must be isolated. When we have ascertained what form the material which he used had, we can discover what changes the Gospel writer made in it. This is comparatively easy with Matthew and Luke. We have in written form one major source—Mark. They also have a great body of other

---

[62] Norman Perrin, *What Is Redaction Criticism?* (Philadelphia: Fortress Press, 1969), p. 25.
[63] Available in English translation in *Tradition and Interpretation in Matthew, op. cit.,* pp. 15-57.
[64] *Op. cit.*
[65] (Nashville: Abingdon, 1969).
[66] H. Stein, "What is *Redaktionsgeschichte?*", *JBL*, 88 (Mar. '69), p. 46.
[67] Rohde, *Rediscovering,* p. 14.
[68] *Ibid.,* p. 45.
[69] *Ibid.,* p. 46.

material in common. By comparing them with Mark and with each other, it is not difficult to discover how they used their material. The case of Mark and John is not so easy. We have no knowledge of their sources and thus we cannot compare the present state of their Gospels with the sources used.

Third, we must analyse the modifications made in the sources and use them as guideposts to the theological concerns of each evangelist. Changes include such things as grouping of material, its arrangement within a geographical and chronological framework, and any alterations within the material itself. Special consideration must be given to such matters as unique material, peculiar vocabulary, Christological titles, and summary statements.[70]

The results of redaction criticism have been by no means unanimously accepted. Though the methods may seem to be scientific, there is still room for the subjective to enter in. It is generally accepted that Conzelmann's designation of Luke as the theologian of salvation history is correct in general. However, it is often noted that the details of his work are too sophisticated to reflect accurately the thought of Luke. It must be remembered that the Gospels were written by common men to common men. They were read aloud and not subjected, in the beginning, to the kind of analytic study which is common today. It would seem that the theological purpose must be found on the surface, readily apparent to the casual listener. It remains true that the first step, the consideration of the gospel as a whole, is the most important step.

The challenge to confidence in the historical trustworthiness of the Gospels that comes from redaction criticism is more apparent than real. Though we must recognize that each Gospel writer made some modifications in his material, this does not mean that the material has been altered in *substance.* The Gospels were written within the context of a believing community. There was no desire to distort the picture of Jesus. The Gospel writers sought to bear testimony to him as he really was. If they had materially altered that picture, they would have been called to judgment by their contemporaries.

The fact that the same Christ of faith emerges from all our Gospels gives us confidence in the essential integrity of our Gospels and the oral tradition that lies behind them. We tend to stress the differences

[70] Rohde, *Rediscovering,* pp. 14-15.

in the Gospels; such undoubtedly exist. But attention should be centered on the unity of the Gospels also. The evangelists do not present four different Christs; they present the same Christ seen from different viewpoints. Their similarities are much more impressive than their differences. Devout men have always been able to go from one Gospel to another without any consciousness of essential change.

In conclusion, the various movements studied have not established any assured results which destroy our confidence in the essential trustworthiness of our Gospels. Some have added to our understanding of the true nature of the Gospels and given us good ground to accept the veracity of the Gospels. It now remains for us to turn to more positive considerations to support our confidence in the reliability of the Gospels.

CHAPTER IV
EVIDENCES FOR THE RELIABILITY OF THE GOSPELS

What speaks for the reliability of the Gospels? Does evidence exist which would give us confidence that they preserve a true picture of Jesus? I think it does. Radical skepticism has been allowed to hold the field without challenge too long. I would agree with Beare that radical skepticism which sees the material in our Gospels as being largely the creation of the Christian communities is unwarranted.[1] Christians did not "produce traditions about Jesus; they reproduced them." [2] I believe it can be shown that the substance of the picture in the Gospels is not distorted, that the Gospels do preserve and transmit a true understanding of what Jesus really was. Admittedly the Gospels are post-Easter interpretations of Jesus, but his interpretation was "in a sense . . . only the *re-discovery* of what had been there in the teaching of Jesus himself." [3]

[1] *Records,* p. 21.
[2] N. A. Dahl, "Kerygma and History" from an excerpt reproduced in *Search* by H. K. McArthur, p. 133.
[3] Moule, *Phenomenon,* p. 46.

My thesis in these two chapters is: *The Gospels transmit the substance of the life and teachings of Jesus reliably.* We will not attempt to show that the Jesus of the Gospels is the Jesus of the technical historian, i.e., a Jesus "unblemished and unembellished by faith and theology," a Jesus based upon evidence that can be verified historically.[4] We only seek to show that the *substance* of the Gospels is not distorted, that the Gospels do preserve a true understanding of Jesus as he "really" was.

As indicated above, we insist that the Gospels are not *mere* historical records. They are historical records of a "higher order."[5] The very fact that each narrator chooses what he will record and omits what does not suit his purpose shows that the Gospels are not objective presentations of history.[6] But this does not mean that history has been distorted. It means that history has been interpreted. It is only through spirit-led interpretation that we know what "really happened."[7]

What do we mean by *substantial truth* as opposed to historically verifiable authenticity? Jeremias has warned us that we must distinguish between a record of the genuine words *(ipsissima verba)* of Jesus and his genuine voice *(ipsissima vox).*[8] The genuine message of Jesus may appear in quite different words than he used. While this is true, the *substance* of what he said is preserved.

To illustrate, we may compare Luke 14:26 with 14:27. In verse 26, we have an authentic saying of Jesus.[9] It reads, "If a man come to me, and hate not his father, and mother, and wife, and children, and brethren, and sisters, yea, and his own life also, he cannot be my disciple." This demand for radical obedience reflects the historical situation of Jesus.

Verse 27 translates that saying into Christian terms: "Whoever does not bear his own cross and come after me, cannot be my disciple" (Cf. Mark 8:34; Matt. 10:38; 16:24; Luke 9:23). Jesus could hardly have used the cross as religious symbol in his own lifetime. The saying reflects the historical situation of the early Christian communities. *But the substance of the two verses is the same.* The terminology is

[4] Braaten, *The Historical Jesus and the Kerygmatic Christ,* p. 81.
[5] Bornkamm *(Jesus,* p. 173) uses this striking phrase for the account of the confession at Caesarea-Philippi. I believe it applies equally well to all the Gospel material.
[6] Schweizer, *Markus,* p. 10.
[7] *Ibid.*
[8] *Theology,* p. 37.
[9] I would not deny that some details have been added (cf. Matt. 10:37), but the main tenor of the saying must be judged to be authentic.

different, but the same demand for radical obedience is preserved. The second, just because it is Christian interpretation, mediates the real Jesus *to us* more clearly than the first. No doubt, the same thing was true of Luke's audience.

Another illustration of the same tendency to translate the substance of a genuine saying of Jesus into the language of early Christianity can be seen by comparing Matthew 10:25 with 23:8. In the first passage, Jesus teaches that a disciple is not above his teacher; it should satisfy him to be like his teacher. In the second, the command reads: "But you are not to be called rabbi (i.e., teacher), for you have one teacher, and you are all brethren." Both passages teach the same thing: discipleship does not lead to promotion to the status of teacher.[10]

A like result comes from comparing Matthew 4:17 with Mark 1:15. Matthew gives what is probably the authentic words of Jesus: "Repent, for the kingdom of heaven is at hand." Mark adds: "and believe in the gospel." Mark's addition translates the demand of Jesus into Christian language. The two sayings are in different words; the substance is the same.

Ernst Fuchs has claimed that the story of the prodigal son is significant for the proclamation of Jesus. He insists that this is true even if the story was created by the community and attributed to Jesus because it is true to Jesus.[11] Higgins rightly remarks that this implies that the authenticity of a saying is secondary; the primary thing is whether it is true to Jesus.[12] I would agree that this is what Fuchs is saying and that it is correct. A saying which is "true" to Jesus is substantially correct even if transmitted in different words.

We must admit that anachronisms exist in the Gospels; we can do nothing else. The wonder is not that there are so many, but that there are so few. Even so, the substance of the story is usually preserved. For instance, John 1:29 pictures John, the Baptist, as introducing Jesus as the "Lamb of God." This expression is unique in the writings of John; it is found nowhere else in the New Testament. Judged from our knowledge of the Baptist's idea and message, this statement would have been impossible to him. This does not mean that it is not a *true* description of what Jesus really was; it means

[10] Bornkamm, *Jesus,* pp. 144-145.
[11] *Studies,* p. 20.
[12] *Tradition,* p. 5.

that it is not an *authentic* report of the actual words of John, the Baptist.

Christian faith asserts that this is a true statement, that Jesus is really the "Lamb of God." But the recognition of this truth did not come until after the resurrection; it was only then that his disciples saw that his death had redemptive significance. The statement of this fact in the figure, "the Lamb of God," is almost certainly a formulation of John, the Evangelist. How then did it come to be placed in the mouth of John, the Baptist? Quite simply! The Baptist had introduced Jesus to his disciples; the Evangelist had come to know him as the Lamb of God. What is more natural than that the Evangelist should put his faith into the mouth of the Baptist? If we are interested in recovering *authentic* words, we must reject this saying. If we are interested in discovering the *true significance* of the earthly Jesus, this may become one of our most valued sayings.

These examples explain why we can say two apparently contradictory things. We can, on the one hand, say that some of the words ascribed to Jesus were not actually his. On the other hand, we can say that the Gospel portrait of Jesus is a true portrait. I would remind you that any life is known in its full dimension only through the verdict of history. We Americans, because history has spoken, are much more sure of our knowledge of men of the remote past (Washington, Jefferson, Lincoln) than of the men of the immediate past or present (Kennedy, Johnson, Nixon). Any life, to be known truly, must be assessed in the light of its total meaning, its outcome, its results. This is true of Jesus also. The verdict of history must become a part of our knowledge of him. The Gospels mediate the words and deeds of Jesus as seen in the light of the resurrection and Christian faith. It is *because* of this, not in spite of it, that we have confidence in their reliability.

Let us now turn to some additional indications of the reliability of the Gospel records. "Indications" is the right word; "proofs" do not exist. No amount of evidence could prove the integrity of the tradition to one who is determined not to believe. But to the believer, the indications are such that he may have confidence that his faith is based on a solid historical foundation. They are enough to give "moral certainty," to remove the events recorded from the "merely possible or probable." [13] These indications put the burden of proof on him who would deny the reliability of the gospel tradition.

1. Indications of Careful Transmission of the Tradition

How was the gospel tradition transmitted? This must be deduced from the evidence. Different scholars make different deductions. Some have insisted that the material is largely a creation of the Christian community. They deny the presence of eyewitnesses to the ministry of Jesus. According to them, the community felt free to alter the material to fit their own needs. They even added material, supposedly from the risen Lord, and this was treated as if it were from the earthly Jesus. [14]

At the opposite pole, two Scandanavian scholars have argued for professional and official methods of transmission. [15] According to them, Jesus taught his disciples and made them memorize his message in the manner of a Jewish rabbi. After his death, Jesus' message was remembered as a "sacred word." The approved guardians and expositors were the apostles. "Ministry of the word" (Acts 6:4) refers to the transmission and development of the holy tradition rather than to proclamation. [16]

The truth of the matter probably lies somewhere between these two extremes. Paul, at least, made a careful distinction between the words of Jesus and the risen Lord speaking through the Spirit (cf. 1 Cor. 7). In answering the Corinthians' questions about marriage, he prefaces his remarks by "I say" twice (vv. 6, 8). Once he says, "I give charge, *not I but the Lord*" (v. 10. Italics mine). Twice he is careful to say that he is not quoting Jesus. "I have no command of the Lord, but I give my opinion" (v. 25. cf. v. 12, "I say, not the Lord.").

In concluding the chapter, Paul asserted: "And I think that I have the Spirit of God" (v. 40). In other words, he felt that all that he said was from the Lord. Some of it came from the risen Lord; some

---

[13] V. Taylor, "Modern Issues in Biblical Studies," *Exp. Times,* 71 (3, '59), pp. 68-72.

[14] Perrin, *Rediscovering,* pp. 15, 30, 31 and Jeremias, *Theology,* p. 2.

[15] H. Riesenfeld, *Gospel Tradition* and Birger Gerhardsson, *Memory and Manuscript (Acts Seminarii Neotestmenici Upsaliensis,* 22; Uppsala, 1961) and *Tradition and Transmission in Early Christianity (Coniectanea Noetestamentica,* 20; Lund, 1964).

[16] Barrett, *Jesus,* p. 18.

of it was based on the teachings of the earthly Jesus. *But he distinguished between them.* Why? Two reasons are probable. One, honesty demanded such a distinction. Two, the Corinthians already knew the tradition of Jesus' words and would know the difference. If Paul was careful to make this distinction, would not others be also?

On the other hand, it is doubtful that there was a professional or official process of transmission.[17] But that a case could be made for such a method is impressive. It shows that there is sufficient evidence of care in transmission on which to base such a view. Davies, though rejecting the view as a whole, believes that it makes it "more historically probably and reasonably credible" that the Gospels contain an authentic picture of Jesus.[18]

We must not suppose that all knowledge of the personal career of Jesus had vanished from the earth when our Gospels were written. Far from it. Many who had walked with him were still alive; there were *eyewitnesses.*[19] Some who had been healed by him were still living. The stories about Jesus had passed by word of mouth from person to person in individual units from the beginning. Generally speaking, no location in time, place, or in the career of Jesus was attached to them. They may have begun like our stories: "Once upon a time." But they were told within a believing community. The memory of the community and its determination to preserve the tradition acted as a constant safeguard against any *substantial* alteration.

In telling and retelling, these stories assumed definite *form;* to this extent the results of form-criticism cannot be denied. Some of them were simple stories of miracles performed; some were stories with a significant saying of Jesus embedded in them; some were remembered sayings of Jesus, perhaps sharpened and repointed to meet the needs of the community. Perhaps the reapplication of the sayings of Jesus is more true of the parables than other sayings. Jesus may have told them in one context with one application while the community told them in another context with another application. We do the same thing in bringing the authority of Jesus to bear on our problems. But, and this is important, we always seek to preserve what Jesus said, not destroy it. The early communities must be supposed to have had the same motive.

[17] Barrett, *Jesus,* p. 18.
[18] W. D. Davies, *Setting of the Sermon on the Mount* (Cambridge: University Press, 1964), p. 480.
[19] Beare, *Records,* p. 21.

We turn now to individual indications of care in the transmission of the tradition. What has been said so far must be remembered; it forms a part of our evidence. From now on our discussion must be atomistic. We cannot place too much weight upon any one point; each is a sort of straw in the wind. The cumulative weight, however, is considerable.

(1) The way in which Matthew and Luke used Markan materials shows care in handling the tradition. Often, the differences between the Gospels are stressed. The impressive thing is their similarities. Both Matthew and Luke used Mark as one of their sources; this is scarcely deniable even today. They also modified Mark in line with their respective purposes; this also is a generally accepted opinion. But how did they modify it? Examination of the evidence shows that they were very careful to preserve the substance of the material; its historical core was retained in the new setting.

For instance, look at the stories of the baptism of Jesus (Mark 1:9-11; Matt. 3:13-17; Luke 3:21-22). Mark, the oldest account, tells us that Jesus was baptized by John the Baptist in Jordan. When he came up out of the water, the heavens were opened. The Spirit of God came down as a dove and rested on Jesus. A voice from heaven said: "Thou art my beloved Son; with thee I am well pleased" (Mark 1:11).

Matthew preserves the story with two changes. He adds, from his special material, an account of the reluctance of the Baptist to baptize Jesus. He pictures the voice as addressing others and saying: "This is my beloved Son, with whom I am well pleased" (3:17).

Luke takes up the story from Mark and tells it with three variations, none of which agrees with Matthew's. He omits the fact that Jesus was baptized by John; he had already recorded John's imprisonment (3:20). He records the fact that Jesus was praying at the time of his baptism. He adds the detail that the Holy Spirit descended in "bodily form" upon Jesus (3:22).

In each case, the essential kernel of the story is preserved. Jesus was baptized; he received the Holy Spirit; the voice from heaven revealed something to him of his mission. The changes made by Matthew and Luke can be ascribed to their theological purposes, *but they did not feel free to change the story itself.*

Matthew wished to stress the sinlessness of Jesus and so he inserted the story of John's reluctance to baptize Jesus. He wanted to stress the fact that the Jews had opportunity to know who Jesus was but rejected him and so the voice is portrayed as addressing them as well as Jesus. Both emphases are true to the historical situation of Jesus' life though neither may belong in this context.

Luke, on the other hand, wishes to focus attention on Jesus himself. For dramatic effect, he places John in prison and omits his part in the baptism. Luke is interested in the prayer life of Jesus and adds the detail that Jesus prayed at his baptism (not at all unbelievable). The addition of the detail that the Spirit descended in "bodily form" only makes explicit what is implicit in Mark. The descent of the Spirit was noted by others as well as Jesus.

This sort of analysis could be repeated a hundred times or more with similar results. In using Markan material, Matthew and Luke were careful to preserve the original kernel of the story or saying as they found it. Such fidelity in their use of one known source, Mark, gives us confidence in their careful use of other materials. Is it too much to suppose that their practice reflects the fidelity of all those who received and handed on the gospel tradition? I think not.

(2) "Foreign" elements in the Gospels give confidence in the care of the transmission of the Jesus-tradition. There are a number of features in the Gospels which are "foreign" to the time in which the Gospels were written. They reflect conditions which were native to the ministry of Jesus. Their retention in the Gospels after a long period of oral transmission is an indication of care in transmitting the tradition.

a. Aramaisms in the Gospels are important in assessing the value of the tradition. Jesus spoke Aramaic; this was his mother tongue.[20] The Gospel writers spoke Greek, wrote in Greek to Greek-speaking readers. Further, their materials were based on traditions which had passed through a period of oral transmission among Greek-speaking communities. Aramaic and Greek are radically different languages; it is possible to discern Aramaic features which have been retained in the process of transmission.[21] The survival of these Aramaic features increases our confidence in the authenticity of our material.[22] They may not lead us back to the voice of Jesus himself, but they do at

[20] So Jeremias (*Theology*, p. 4) and the majority of scholars. But H. P. Rüger (*"Zum Problem der Sprache Jesu,"* ZNTW, 59, 1968, pp. 113-122) questions this as an assured fact. He thinks Jesus spoke Hebrew as well.

[21] Perrin, *Rediscovering*, p. 37.

[22] Fuller, *Current Study*, p. 33.

least prove that "an Aramaic sayings-source or tradition lies behind the Synoptic Gospels." [23] The retention of these features shows a more-than-ordinary fidelity to the sources. It certainly shows that the evangelists were not "freely inventing" material.[24]

(a) There are a number of *Aramaic words and expressions* which have been taken over into the tradition without change, i.e., the Aramaic word was simply spelled with Greek letters. One well-known instance is *Talitha Cumi* which Mark retains though it must be translated for his audience: "little girl, I say to you, Arise" (Mark 5:41). Another is *Ephphatha* which Mark translates as "be opened" (Mark 7:34). The cry of Jesus from the cross is also preserved in both its Aramaic original and a Greek translation: "*Eli, Eli, Lama sabackthani?*" which means, "My God, My God, why has thou forsaken me?" (Matt. 27:46; cf. Mark 15:34).

Jeremias lists nineteen Aramaic words which have been preserved in the Gospels.[25] He adds that the underlying Aramaic wording can be discerned in "many (additional) passages," [26] including those which are at home in Aramaic but alien to both Greek and Hebrew. He rightly concludes that discovery of the Aramaic background of the sayings of Jesus is "of great significance in assessing the reliability of the gospels." [27]

(b) *Aramaic ways of speaking* abound in the tradition preserved in the Gospels. When the teachings of Jesus are compared with the characteristic way of speaking by his contemporaries, the number of Aramaisms which occur on his lips are striking both in their number and variety.[28]

Circumlocutions for God are especially prevalent. Jeremias lists eighteen of these, many used very often.[29] Especially interesting is Jesus' habit of using what is called the "divine passive," i.e., the passive voice used to speak of an action of God. For example, "To you has been given the secret of the kingdom of God" (Mark 4:11) obviously means that God has given them the secret. Jeremias finds about one hundred occurrences of this type of passive, distributed as follows:

[23] Matthew Black, *An Aramaic Approach to the Gospels and Acts* (Oxford: Clarendon Press, 3rd Ed., 1967), p. 271.
[24] Barrett, *Jesus,* p. 6.
[25] *Theology,* pp. 5-6.
[26] *Ibid.,* p. 6.
[27] *Ibid.,* p. 8.
[28] *Ibid.,* pp. 9-10. See also Black, *Aramaic Background,* for a fuller discussion of these features.
[29] *Ibid.*

twenty-one in Mark, twenty-three in material common to Matthew and Luke, twenty-seven in Matthew's special material, and twenty-five in Luke's special material.[30]

This is striking indeed, especially in view of the fact that this type of passive is very rare in Talmudic literature. It must have been a feature of Jesus' own way of speaking.[31] The preservation of so many instances in our Gospels indicates how persistently Jesus' way of speaking was retained in the transmission of tradition.

Antithetic parallelism is another Aramaic characteristic of the teaching of Jesus; it is found in all strata of the tradition (Mark, thirty times, thirty-four in material common to Matthew and Luke, forty-four in Matthew, and thirty in Luke). Though this was not unique with Jesus, being found also in the Old Testament and in the Judaism of Jesus' day, Jesus used it with a "versatility that is noteworthy." [32] The frequency of the usage shows that it is derived from Jesus' own way of speaking.[33]

Various types of rhythm are also found in the sayings of Jesus when translated back into Aramaic.[34] Both the Greek and English translations of the Gospels obscure this characteristic of Jewish poetry, but it abounds in many rhythmic patterns. This indicates that we are dealing with a characteristic way in which Jesus taught.[35] Even if this is not admitted, it does indicate a Semitic background and shows the antiquity of the tradition preserved in the Gospels.

Alliteration, assonance, and paronomasia are also present to an unusual degree in the teachings of Jesus when these are translated back into Aramaic.[36] Most of these rhetorical forms are lost in translation. However, even the English translation of Mark 9:50 preserves the alliteration which was in the original Aramaic: "If the salt has lost its saltness, how will you season it?"

In conclusion, no one example of Aramaism is impressive. But when one considers the cumulative effect of all of them, he cannot fail to find them striking. He is almost forced to believe that they represent the authentic voice of Jesus. Their retention in our Gospels adds to our confidence in the integrity of the transmission of the tradition.

[30] *Ibid.,* p. 11.
[31] Perrin, *Rediscovering,* p. 38.
[32] Jeremias, *Theology,* p. 19.
[33] *Ibid.,* p. 18.
[34] C. F. Burney, *The Poetry of Our Lord* (Oxford: Clarendon, 1925), pp. 100-146.
[35] Jeremias, *Theology,* p. 27.
[36] *Ibid.,* pp. 27-29 and Black, *Aramaic Background,* pp. 160-185.

b. The retention of rhetorical forms unique with Jesus adds to our confidence in the Gospels. There are two forms of teaching which are quite frequent in the teaching of Jesus but which have no analogy in contemporary literature. Neither are to be found in early Christian literature nor in rabbinic teaching. Therefore, they may be said to be genuine characteristics of Jesus' method of teaching.

Parables are a teaching method almost unique with Jesus (no less than forty-one are found in the Synoptics). Nothing in Judaism, Essene writings, Pauline, or rabbinic literature compares with them.[37] Even the Old Testament has only scattered examples (cf. 2 Sam. 12:1-7; Isa. 5:1-7; Hos. 11). The parables represent the "most markedly individualistic characteristic of the teaching of Jesus."[38] They belong to the "bedrock" of the Jesus-tradition.[39] Their number and originality in content and form stamps them with the personality of Jesus.[40] The fact that the Gospels have preserved so many of them and have made them the chief vehicle of Jesus' teaching should give us confidence in the integrity of the Gospel materials.

Riddles are not rare in the teaching of Jesus but almost unheard of in other teachers of that day and in the rest of the New Testament.[41] Some of Jesus' riddles are still difficult to explain; they were mysterious sayings to outsiders in his own day. They include: the saying about John the Baptist (Matt. 11:11), about the old and the new (Mark 2:21-22), about the fate of Jesus (Mark 9:31), about Elijah (Mark 9:11), about the three days (Luke 13:32-33), and about the three kinds of eunuch (Matt. 19:12).[42]

c. Retention of the distinctive vocabulary of Jesus shows that the tradition was not lightly changed in its transmission.

Abba as a form of address to God was unique with Jesus. Jeremias argues convincingly that it is "the most important linguistic innovation" Jesus made.[43] *Abba* is derived from the chatter of children and reveals a most intimate fellowship with God.[44] Such intimacy of address would have shocked pious Jews. True, they sometimes addressed God

[37] Jeremias, *Theology, p. 29.*
[38] Perrin, *Rediscovering,* p. 22.
[39] Jeremias, *Theology,* p. 30.
[40] Perrin, *Rediscovering,* p. 29.
[41] Jeremias, *Theology,* pp. 30-31.
[42] *Ibid.*
[43] *Theology,* p. 36. Compare with his, *The Prayers of Jesus* (London: SCM Press, 1967), pp. 11-64 and W. G. Kümmel, *Promise and Fulfillment* (London: SCM, 1956), p. 36.
[44] Jeremias, *Prayers,* p. 111.

as Father but always with some additional phrase such as, "who is in heaven," used to emphasize his transcendence.[45] All strata of the Jesus-tradition testifies that Jesus addressed God as "my Father" and that he always did this in his prayers.[46] *Abba* is preserved only in Mark 14:36, but it probably lies behind the other instances which are preserved only in the Greek translation.[47] We can reasonably conclude that the use of *Abba* as an address to God is unique with Jesus.

"*Amen*" is used in a new way in the Gospels. Among the Jews, the word was always used to give assent to what others said. Jesus used it to preface his own sayings; it served to introduce and strengthen his message. The usage is confined entirely to Jesus' own words in the Gospels, in Mark thirteen times, in material common to Matthew and Luke nine, in Matthew's special material nine and in Luke's special material three. John, in his twenty-five uses, always doubles the word.[48] The retention of this alien word in the tradition, the way in which its use is restricted to Jesus, and the fact that all strata of the tradition testify to its use shows that we have "the creation of a new expression by Jesus."[49]

The Son of man as a self-designation is found in our Gospels about eighty times.[50] With one exception (Acts 7:56), it is found nowhere else in the New Testament. This seems to be a genuine reminiscence of the teaching of Jesus.[51] If a "Son of man theology" had arisen in the early churches as some assert, it is hardly conceivable that the title would never have been used to address Jesus nor found any echo in the epistles. Evidently the early churches never had a doctrine of the Son of man; it must be accepted as Jesus' own favorite term for himself.[52]

Disciple as a designation of the followers of Jesus is confined to the Gospels and Acts; it is not found in any of the epistles (forty-six times in Mark, seventy-eight in Matthew, thirty-seven in Luke, seventy-eight in John, and twenty-eight in Acts). Its place is taken in the epistles by such terms as "saints," believers," and the "elect."

[45] G. Kittel, *"Abba," TDNT*, V. 1, p. 5.
[46] Jeremias (*Theology*, p. 62) lists sixteen instances in the four Gospels.
[47] Kittel, *op. cit.*, p. 6.
[48] Jeremias, *Theology*, p. 35. Compare with Perrin, *Rediscovering*, p. 38.
[49] Jeremias, *Theology*, p. 36.
[50] Reumann, *Jesus*, p. 267.
[51] Barrett, *Jesus*, p. 6.
[52] E. Stauffer, *The Story of Jesus*, p. 163.

Disciple was a proper designation for the followers of the earthly Jesus; it was soon replaced by other terms which would more properly describe the devotees of the risen Lord.

Saints, the favorite designation for Christians in the epistles, is found only in Matthew 27:52 as a designation of the followers of Jesus. This designation belonged to the post-resurrection community. The preservation of the distinction between "disciple" and "saints" shows a finer historical sense in the Gospels than most scholars admit.

Kingdom (Grk., *Basileia*) is, according to the Gospels, used by Jesus in a unique way. The word occurs on his lips thirteen times in Mark, nine in material common to Matthew and Luke, twenty-seven in special Matthean material, and twelve is special Lukan material.[53] It occurs only rarely in the rest of the New Testament, almost always with a meaning which was not the most characteristic with Jesus. Jeremias has compiled a list of phrases which Jesus used in relation to the kingdom which have no parallels, not even secular ones, in the language of Jesus' day.[54] The most striking are: The kingdom "has come near" (Mark 1:15), "has come upon you" (Matt. 12:28), "is seized" and has "suffered violence" (Matt. 11:12), is "within (or among") you" (Luke 17:21). This is all new language. Its inclusion in the Gospels shows a remarkable fidelity to the actual words of Jesus.

Obedience (Grk., *upakoe, upakoein*) is rarely found in the gospels; it is often found in Paul's writings. Aramaic had no word for obedience; the idea was expressed indirectly by such words as "to hear," "to keep," and "to do."[55] If the Gospel material had been freely produced in the Christian communities, the Greek words for obey would undoubtedly have been common since the idea is common. Yet the noun is never found, and the verb occurs only three times (when parallels are eliminated).

Called is used in an entirely different sense in Jesus' teachings and Paul's letters. For Jesus, the word meant an invitation to share in God's forgiveness. Thus, he could say, "Many are called, but few are chosen" (Matt. 22:14). For Paul, it meant more than that; it meant an effective call to salvation. For him all who were called were saved.

[53] Jeremias, *Theology,* p. 32.
[54] *Ibid.,* pp. 33-34.
[55] Reinhard Deichbräger, *"Gehorsam and Gehorchen in der Verkundigung Jesu,"* ZNTW, 1/2, 1961, p. 119.

The fidelity of the Gospels to Jesus' word usage is another straw in the wind that indicates careful transmission of the tradition.

In conclusion, these phenomena of vocabulary are striking in their cumulative effect. New Testament scholarship will no doubt find other instances. Of itself, this evidence might not be judged convincing. When added to other evidence, it tends to add weight to our contention that the Gospels have preserved the *substance* of Jesus' teachings intact.

(3) "Embarrassing" elements in the Gospels reflect the care with which tradition was transmitted. Moule suggests that some elements must be genuine since "everything else was hostile to their survival." [56] Some seemingly reflect on the dignity and divinity of Jesus, others on the character of the apostles.

The baptism of Jesus is one such element. The account of Jesus' baptism at the hands of the Baptist became a difficult and scandalous problem in early Christian circles. This was due to the emergence of a Baptist movement in competition with the Christian movement. His baptism leaves the door open to the charge that Jesus was inferior to John. "This is history as it happened." [57]

The temptations of Jesus seem, on the surface, to challenge the Christian conception of Jesus as sinless. The survival of the accounts indicate their genuineness.

That Jesus' friends thought him mad (Mark 3:21) would certainly not have survived unless it was genuine.

Jesus' question to the young ruler (Mark 10:18), "Why do you call me good? No one is good but God alone" is a question that no Christian would have invented.

Nor would any Christian have dared to picture Jesus *as being ignorant of a future event.* Yet the Gospels preserve his saying that he did not know the time of the end (Mark 13:32).

Jesus' prayer in Gethsemane seems to run counter to the Christian idea that Jesus went to the cross voluntarily. It can be explained, but it seems paradoxical. It is difficult to believe that this account was invented by Christians.

The cry of dereliction from the cross (Mark 15:34) is another bit of tradition which might be called "embarrassing" to the Christian movement. It is hardly likely that it is an invented story. Both John and Luke omit the account.

[56] *Phenomenon,* p. 62.
[57] Barrett, *Jesus,* p. 5.

Reflections against Peter also exist in the tradition. These are not as "embarrassing" as reflections against Christ, but it is highly unlikely that they would have been invented. Peter is pictured as being the spokesman of Satan at Caesarea-Philippi (Mark 8:32-33). He is said to have suggested the building of three tabernacles on the mountain in honor of Jesus, Elijah, and Moses. Mark adds that he did not know what he was saying (Mark 9:6; cf. Luke 9:33). The story of Peter's denial of Jesus is embedded in the passion story, though not essential to it (Mark 14:53-72 and parallels).

These "embarrassing" elements in the Gospels certainly increase our confidence in the integrity of the transmission of the Jesus-tradition. Their retention shows that the men who handled the tradition sought to preserve it without *essential change.*

(4) The preservation of the situation of Jesus' time reflects care in transmission. Form critics have often asserted that the Gospel material reflects the *"sitz-im-leben"* of the early Christian communities rather than that of Jesus. This is certainly not always true; there are a number of instances in the Gospels where the situation in life of Jesus' own day is preserved (including some discussed above).

a. True details of Palestinian life are often reflected in Jesus' parables and in some of the stories about him. This indicates that the Gospels are based on Semitic and Palestinian material.[58] Instead of reading their own life situation back into the material, the Gospel writers passed the tradition on as they found it.

b. A comparison of Luke and Acts shows that Luke was careful not to blur the distinction between the situation of Jesus and that of early Christianity. Luke wrote both books; yet, he is careful to preserve with care and consistency the distinction between what people thought of Jesus before and after his resurrection.[59]

The difference in the use of Lord as a title for Jesus in the two books is impressive. After the resurrection, "Lord" is natural to the disciples as a title for Jesus (Luke 24:34). This use is quite common in Acts. Not so in the Gospel. When we eliminate the vocative (no more meaningful than our common, "dear sir" to open a letter) and Luke's editorial remarks, it is rare to find participants in the story referring to Jesus as "Lord." In the birth stories, it is used by Elizabeth (Luke 1:43), Zachariah (Luke 1:76), and the angels (Luke 2:11). Even

---

[58] *Ibid.,* p. 6.
[59] See Moule (*Phenomenon,* pp. 57-61) for a detailed discussion of this matter.

so, these do not constitute an application of the title to the man Jesus. The only other possible exception is in Jesus' instruction about the colt which the disciples repeated to its owner (Luke 19:31,34). This evidence shows that Luke was careful not to read the Christian title for the risen Christ back into the preresurrection ministry of Jesus.

Prophet is applied to Jesus in both books, but with a subtle distinction.[60] In Acts, Jesus is *"the* Prophet like Moses" (Acts 3:22; cf. Deut. 18:15). In no other sense is he called a prophet. In the Gospel, Jesus alludes to himself as being among the prophets (4:24; 13:33). He is also called *a* prophet by the disbelievers and the disillusioned (7:16,39; 9:8,19; 24:19). In the use of this word, the distinction between the pre- and postresurrection Jesus has been carefully preserved.

Savior appears in the Gospel only on the lips of the angel (Luke 2:11). In Acts, his name is the only one through whom salvation comes (Acts 4:12). Both Peter (Acts 5:31) and Paul (Acts 13:23) explicitly call him Savior.[61]

Son of God is used in the Gospel only by other than "human voices," (Luke 1:32,35; 3:22; 4:3,9,41; 8:28) and by Jesus himself (Luke 10:22; 22:70).[62] In Acts, Paul explicitly used the title for Jesus (Acts 9:20; 13:33).

The Son of man appears in the Gospel only on the lips of Jesus. In Acts, it appears only once, on the lips of the dying Stephen (Acts 7:56).[63]

Jesus himself, in the Gospel, is especially endowed with *the Holy Spirit* (cf. also the miniature gospel in Acts 10). In Acts, Jesus pours out the Holy Spirit on his followers (cf. Acts 2:33).[64]

I would agree with Moule that the evidences of the "differences in continuity" are not artificial but preserve the true distinction between the pre- and postresurrection ministries of Jesus.[65] After the resurrection, Jesus is seen as a transcendent being; before it, he was seen as a specially-endowed human personality. Luke has preserved this distinction in his two books. This fact tends to deepen our confidence in the integrity of our Gospels.

c. *A comparison of the Gospels and the Epistles* reveals the same

[60] *Ibid.,* p. 59.
[61] *Ibid.*
[62] *Ibid.*
[63] *Ibid.,* p. 60.
[64] *Ibid.,* p. 61.
[65] *Ibid.*

care in preserving the distinction between the pre- and postresurrection Jesus. Howard M. Teeple vigorously states that there was never an authentic tradition of the words of Jesus.[66] He insists that the flow of ideas was not from Jesus to the apostles, but the reverse, i.e., the words of the apostles were read back into the mouth of the earthly Jesus.[67] To support his contentions, Teeple points out: (1) that Jesus' teachings are rarely quoted outside the Gospels; (2) that Jesus' view of the Jewish law is not shared by Paul and John; (3) that Jesus is not quoted concerning vital problems of the early Christians, such as the delay of the parousia and the persecution of the Christians; (4) that Christian literature is quite varied in form; and (5) that the Holy Spirit, not Jesus, was considered the ultimate authority within the Christian movement.[68]

Teeple's statements may be provisionally accepted, but they disprove rather than prove his thesis. The evidence indicates that Jesus taught his disciples in ways that were relevant to the situation in his own life. His exact words were not necessarily relevant to the life of the Christian communities. Often the situation had changed. The apostles ministered to the Christian communities under the leadership of the Holy Spirit. They dealt with the problems of these communities in a creative way, not contradicting Jesus, but supplementing and applying his teaching from words of the risen Christ.

The very fact that we do not have uniformity between the Epistles and the recorded words of Jesus argues that the Gospels preserve the substance of Jesus' teaching. It certainly does not indicate that they read words back into the mouth of Jesus which originated with the Apostles.

d. The different directions of the mission of Jesus and the churches show fidelity to the different situations in life. The mission of Jesus was limited to Israel. In the Synoptics, no hint of a mission to the Gentiles is found during Jesus' lifetime.[69] In Acts and the Epistles, the mission is twofold. The Jews are not forgotten, but the Gentiles become the primary target. The churches felt that the Gentile mission was a legitimate extension of Jesus' teaching. It was, but the Gospels are remarkably consistent in retaining a sense of historical reality in reporting Jesus' ministry.

[66] "The Oral Tradition that Never Existed," *JBL* 86 (March, 1970), pp. 56-68.
[67] *Ibid.*, p. 61.
[68] *Ibid.*, pp. 63-66.
[69] Jeremias, *Theology*, p. 245.

2. The Gospels Make Sense

Subjective opinions are of little value in making historical judgments, yet they are not entirely without meaning. If it can be shown that the Gospels as they stand make sense while the reconstructions of radical critics do not, this should be noted. If true, this should increase our confidence in the *substantial* reliability of the Gospels. They do make sense; they present a coherent picture of Jesus; they explain why he was killed; and, they explain why the Christian movement arose.

(1) The Gospel portrait of Jesus is coherent. The picture of Jesus is so coherent and consistent within itself that it is inconceivable that it is an invented picture.[70] Jesus, as he stands in the Gospels, is unique. He conforms to none of the religious figures of Israel or of the world. Similarities exist between him and the prophets, the teachers, or the apocalyptists. But if one tries to fit him into any mold, he soon finds that the mold falls far short of explaining him. Jewish figures, such as the Prophet like Moses, the Messiah, or the Suffering Servant, were used to point to the continuity of Jesus with the past. Yet, none of these, *as conceived in the Jewish mind,* explain him. Starting from them, no one could have invented Jesus. Rather, his career took up these figures and transformed them to fit into the reality of his life.

(2) The Gospel portrait explains why Jesus died. One fact of history is that Jesus was executed on a Roman cross. Why? Liberal scholars of the nineteenth century had no adequate explanation; their devout and lovable teacher of morals could not possibly have been crucified.[71] Modern existentialists have constructed a different picture, a picture of a prophet and rabbi, a "voice before the end." Is it any more likely that such a one would have been executed on a Roman cross? I think not.

The Gospels are not concerned with tracing the cause of his death; they are concerned with describing his death as a saving event.[72] However, they do give a clue that makes sense. He was understood to be a messianic pretender, a potential threat to Roman power. This explains why the Jews thought him a blasphemer and conspired to put him to death. This explains why Rome could be persuaded to

[70] Moule, *Phenomenon,* pp. 77-78.
[71] Betz, *Know,* p. 83.
[72] Dahl, *Kerygma and History,* p. 137 in *Search,* by McArthur.

crucify him. The official reason for his death is contained in the superscription on the cross: "The King of the Jews" (Mark 15:26).

(3) The Gospels explain why the Christian movement arose; nothing else does. It is an uncontested fact of history that soon after Jesus' death his disciples proclaimed his resurrection, acknowledged him as the Savior of men, and began to worship him as their living leader. Any theory about the Gospels must account for this fact. Yet, there is no purely "historical, non-transcendental event" that explains this phenomenon.[73]

The explanation of the resurrection faith and the rise of the Christian movement must be sought in fact. The reason cannot be found in the personality of Jesus; other men of the same period could have pointed to a more illustrative career—Hillel, Judas Maccabees, The Teacher of Righteousness. Yet, none of these men were proclaimed as risen from the dead. They were simply dead heroes whose memory was cherished. The explanation cannot be found in the gullibility of the disciples. They came to faith by the roadway of doubt. Their previous experiences and the tenets of their religion were against it. They had to be persuaded.

The simplest and most sensible explanation is to suppose that the Gospel records are reliable. The disciples did experience the risen Christ. What the Gospels teach as true is true. The radical change in the disciples between Calvary and Pentecost is easily explained by supposing the reality of Easter; it is impossible to explain on any other grounds.

---

[73] Moule, *Phenomenon*, p. 77.

CHAPTER V
JESUS' SELF-UNDER-STANDING

What did Jesus think about himself? This is one of the most confused areas of New Testament study today. Of course what he thought of himself is not determinative for Christian faith. He could have thought of himself as the Messiah without being so; he could have been so without thinking of himself as such. The important thing to Christian faith is that he was the Messiah in *actual fact,* i.e., that his ministry was the climax of God's redemptive act, that through him men may receive forgiveness of sins.

It is important, however, to inquire about Jesus' own self-understanding. If it can be shown that the Gospel presentation is correct at this point, it adds tremendously to our confidence in the reliability of the Gospels. Our attention in the last chapter was focused on many particular points. Jesus' self-understanding includes a whole strand of thought that is woven into the fabric of the Gospels. If the Gospels are true at this point, it is probable that they are true at all points.

The usual approach to the question of Jesus' self-understanding has been to investigate his use or acceptance of various titles—Messiah, Son of man, Son of God. This seems to be a wrong direction for two reasons. *One,* it is impossible to be sure that Jesus did or did not use any of these titles. *Two,* these titles did not have any definite or definable meaning in the Judaism of Jesus' day. At least, scholars cannot agree on the meaning they had. They came to have definite meaning in Christian theology, but this came about by reading back into them what Jesus was rather than by the reverse process. Thus, even if we could establish that Jesus used the titles, they would tell us little of the content of his self-understanding.

Where then shall we turn? There is an increasing recognition that we must turn to the implications of his message, conduct, and demands. Perrin has praised Bultmann for raising the question of Jesus' consciousness in a challenging and fruitful manner, i.e., by inquiring into the significance of his message.[1] Fuchs has insisted that the conduct of Jesus is the real framework of his proclamation.[2] I think this is fundamentally the right approach. It works with others; why not with Jesus? Any man's self-understanding is revealed more clearly by his implicit than by his explicit claims. What Jesus thought of himself will be more clearly revealed by what he said about other things than by what he said about himself.

My thesis in this chapter will be: *The self-understanding attributed to Jesus by the Gospels is authentic in its substance.* By this, I mean that Jesus implicitly and indirectly claimed for himself the status which the Gospels indicate. It *may* be that he did not do so by accepting or using the titles which the Gospels attribute to him. The presence of the titles in the tradition *could* be a reading back into his lifetime of postresurrection usage. Even so, these titles are the only categories which would have done "justice to his claim." [3]

We will look first at the implicit claims of Jesus as they are seen in his exercise of absolute authority, his sense of vocation, and his teaching on the fatherhood of God. This portion of our study will be based only on passages which can reasonably be labeled authentic. Then we will look at the explicit claims attributed to him in the Gospels and ask whether these are any more exalted then the implicit claims.

[1] N. Perrin, *The Kingdom of God in the Teaching of Jesus* (London: SCM Press, 1963), p. 119.
[2] *Studies,* p. 21.
[3] Käsemann, *Essays,* p. 38.

If we find that they are harmonious with each other, we will consider that the Gospel presentation of Jesus' self-understanding is valid.

1. The Implicit Claims of Jesus

The message and conduct of Jesus necessarily imply a number of claims to an exalted status, a unique position, among men. In the passages now under consideration, he never says in so many words that he speaks and acts for God, but he implies this. He never says that his ministry is eschatological in meaning, but he implies this. He never says that he is uniquely the Son of God, but he implies this.

(1) Jesus exercised an absolute authority in his ministry. He acted and spoke as one who "himself stood in God's place," [4] "opens up immediacy to God," [5] and had "divine authority." [6] Harvey points out that this argument for a continuity between Jesus and the proclamation of the church is employed in one way or another by Bornkamm, Conzelmann, Ebeling, Fuchs, and Käsemann. This implied claim of authority "sets him apart from the Jewish environment." [7]

a. An implied claim to absolute authority is contained in the *antitheses of the Sermon on the Mount* as given in Matthew. The form of the antitheses is: "You have heard that it was said to men of old . . . But I say to you." Six of these statements are found in Matthew 5 (21 f., 27 f., 31 f., 33 f., 38 f., and 43 f.). It is generally accepted that these antitheses represent an authentic strand in the teaching of Jesus. They certainly do not reflect the practice of Judaism. No Jewish rabbi could have used them. If one had done so, he would have cut himself off from the community or been accused of claiming to be the Messiah.[8] No Christian would have felt constrained to invent the saying. In early Christianity the authority of Jesus was accepted without question. They must be attributed to Jesus and be recognized as an implicit claim to an authority that superseded that of Moses and the Law.

b. *Jesus' use of "Amen" implies a claim to direct authority.* The way in which Jesus used the words is a "completely new manner of speak-

---

[4] Fuchs, *Studies,* pp. 21-22.
[5] Conzelmann, *Outline,* p. 127.
[6] Jeremias, *Prayers,* p. 115.
[7] Harvey, *Historian,* p. 175.
[8] Käsemann, *Essays,* p. 37.

ing."[9] Placing the "Amen" before his sayings implies "his total engagement to the act of God."[10] The implication of the term, so used, is that the words of Jesus are "reliable and true" just because Jesus said them.[11] For this reason, we can regard Jesus' use of the term as a claim to authority that is divine in origin.[12] This is why it can be said that the term involves a whole Christology in a nutshell.[13]

The least that can be said about Jesus' use of "Amen" is that it implies a self-understanding that transcends that of any of the religious leaders of Israel—lawgivers, prophets, teachers. They all spoke, not in their own name, but in the name of God. Though Jesus did not disassociate himself from God, he spoke in the first person as one who was invested with full authority.

c. *Jesus' modification and change of the Old Testament* law implied his right to exercise absolute authority. Other rabbis sought to interpret the law with relevancy, but insisted that the law was the highest authority. While they often twisted the law to fit their exegesis, they always sought to show that their interpretation was an *interpretation* and not a change of the law.

Jesus, on the other hand, did not hesitate to challenge the law itself. We have already noticed the antitheses of the Sermon on the Mount, but these do not exhaust the material. For instance, he attacked the purification laws of the Jews (Mark 7:1-23; Matt. 15:1-20). He denied that men could be defiled in his essential being by anything from the outside. For Jesus, the decisive matter is the heart of man; from it procedes either good or evil. Salvation and true worship mean that the heart must be made to conform to God's will. In saying this, Jesus removed the distinction between the sacred and secular. He struck a death blow at the Jewish cultus and challenged the hitherto unchallenged authority of Moses.[14]

Jesus also swept away the permission for divorce which Moses, he said, had allowed because of the hardness of men's hearts (Mark 10:1-12; Matt. 19:1-12). Though he based his conclusions on Scripture, referring the matter back to God's intention in creation, he challenged the authority of Moses. He made his own teaching superior to the

[9] Jeremias, *Prayers,* p. 112.
[10] Fuller, *Study,* p. 35.
[11] Heinrich Schlier, "Amen," *TDNT,* V. 1, p. 338.
[12] Käsemann, *Essays,* pp. 41-42.
[13] Schlier, *op. cit.*
[14] Käsemann, *Essays,* p. 39.

law. This was equivalent to saying that he was the "instrument of that Living Spirit of God which Judaism expected to be the gift of the End." [15]

Jesus' challenge to the sabbath laws (Mark 2:23 to 3:6 and parallels) points in the same direction. In challenging them, Jesus spoke as a man must speak "if he were in God's place." [16]

d. *The conduct of Jesus contained an implied claim to absolute authority.* Jesus dared to fly in the face of all the attitudes of the Jews toward outcasts. Particularly noteworthy was his habit of associating with tax collectors and sinners (cf. Luke 15:1, etc.). This element in the conduct of Jesus is attested so widely that its authenticity can hardly be doubted. Ernst Fuchs has been most insistent about the importance of the conduct of Jesus as a sign of his own self-understanding. He feels that it is more important than miracle stories or the use of titles for Jesus. He insists that the conduct of Jesus was that of a man "who dares to act in God's stead." [17]

e. The *demand of Jesus for radical obedience* presumed the right to command them absolutely. His demand was often couched in terms of hating father and family (Luke 14:26). It was also stated in many other ways.[18] The point is that he commanded them to render unto him absolute obedience and this demand implied a consciousness on his part of the right to command. He told them that when they had done "all that is commanded you," they had only done their "duty" (Luke 17:10).

I think these points are sufficient to show that Jesus exercised an absolute authority in his ministry. We must view this as a usurpation of an authority that was not properly his or recognize that the early Christians were correct in insisting that it was rightfully his. In either case, there is no question that his self-understanding was such that it had to be translated into the very terms which the Christians used to describe his person. No other terms were adequate as vehicles to communicate his self-understanding.

(2) Jesus interpreted his mission eschatologically, that is, as having ultimate meaning for both time and eternity. Such an interpretation would not be proper to an ordinary man, not even to a prophet of Israel.

[15] *Ibid.,* p. 42.
[16] Fuchs, *Studies,* p. 21.
[17] *Ibid.,* pp. 21, 22.
[18] See Chapter 7 on discipleship.

First, we notice that Jesus associated the coming of the kingdom of God and salvation for men with his own person. He said, "If I by the finger of God am casting out demons; then has come the kingdom of God upon you" (Luke 11:20; cf. Matt. 12:28). Jesus interpreted the success of his actions as a sign that the kingdom of God had already come, that it was actually present in his ministry.[19] In Jesus something unique in history had begun and the sovereign power of God had come "into effective operation."[20]

The saying: "He who is not with me is against me" (Luke 11:23; Matt. 12:30) points to the ultimate significance of Jesus' person and ministry. It implies that the destiny of every man is decided by his decision about Jesus.

The two similes of the patched garment and the new wine in old wineskins (Mark 2:21-22) asserts that Jesus' ministry was "quite incompatible with the existing categories of Judaism."[21]

The claim of Jesus that the prophecy of Isaiah 61:1-2 was fulfilled in his own person (Luke 4:21) announced that the final drama of redemption had already begun in his life.[22]

These passages are sufficient to show beyond question that Jesus believed that the kingdom had already come in his own work.[23] This implies clearly that Jesus understood himself in the same way in which the postresurrection Christology pictured him.[24] His conception of himself is "included in the Messianic titles given him by the Church."[25]

Another strand of teachings which shows Jesus' understanding of his ministry are those sayings which might be called the "I cames" of Jesus.[26] In these passages, all of them in the past tense, Jesus said that he came: to cast fire on the earth (Luke 12:49), not to bring peace but a sword (Matt. 10:34; Luke 12:51), to turn family members against one another (Matt. 10:35; Luke 12:52), to fulfil the law and the prophets (Matt. 5:17), to call sinners to repentance (Mark 2:17), to serve and give his life a ransom for many (Mark 10:45), to seek and save the lost (Luke 19:10), and to preach throughout Israel (Mark

---

[19] See next chapter for a fuller discussion.
[20] C. H. Dodd, *The Parables of the Kingdom* (New York: Scribner's, Revised Edition, 1961), p. 29.
[21] Perrin, *Understanding*, p. 81.
[22] John Bright, *The Kingdom of God in Bible and Church* (London: Lutterworth, 1955), p. 201.
[23] Käsemann, *Essays*, p. 43.
[24] Conzelmann, *Outline*, p. 140.
[25] Bornkamm, *Jesus*, p. 174.
[26] J. A. T. Robinson, *Jesus and His Coming* (Nashville: Abingdon, 1957), p. 63.

1:38). This list is striking. It points to a consciousness of eschatological significance for his ministry on Jesus' part.

Another fact that *may* be significant is that Jesus chose twelve disciples instead of eleven. Moule sees in this fact "an implicit Christology of great height." [27] If the twelve are taken to be representative of new Israel, Jesus put himself, not within, but above and outside Israel as its Lord.

(3) Jesus' use of Abba shows a consciousness of unique sonship. There is little room to question the fact that Jesus did use *Abba* as a form of address to God and that this represents an innovation on his part.[28] It is striking also that Jesus never joins himself with the disciples in saying, "Our Father." He speaks to them of "your Father"; he, himself, calls God either "Father" or "my Father." [29]

What does this mean? Bornkamm is right, I think, in saying that the messianic titles given to Jesus by Christians rests upon Jesus' self-understanding of the "unique character of his relationship to the Father." [30]

In the light of this evidence of the unique self-understanding of Jesus, we must conclude that the early Christian Christology is based on solid historical fact, i.e., Jesus thought of himself in ways which for them could only be characterized by the use of Messiah or Son of God. No title, no matter how exalted, could surpass in content what is implicit in the words and conduct of Jesus.

There had to be some reason for the faith of the disciples. It is unique in the history of religion. For a group of men to come to believe that their teacher, now dead, has actually risen from the grave and is their living Lord is unheard of in any other religion. If their confession, "Jesus is the Christ," does not stem from the self-understanding of Jesus, where did it come from? How could it arise? The only answer that makes good sense is to suppose that the disciples were perpetuating a belief which is based on Jesus' own self-understanding. This is true whether or not we decide that Jesus did or did not use the term Messiah. It was the only available valid category to use in response to his claims.[31]

[27] *Phenomenon*, pp. 68-69.
[28] Jeremias, *Prayers*, pp. 11-65 and Perrin, *Rediscovering*, p. 174 and discussion in previous chapter.
[29] Conzelmann (*Outline*, p. 102) argues that this distinction arose in the church and is not original with Jesus, but his arguments are unconvincing.
[30] *Jesus*, p. 174.
[31] Perrin, *Kingdom*, p. 125.

2. The Alleged Explicit Claims of Jesus

In the light of the implicit claims of Jesus, we may now turn to the alleged explicit claims contained in the Gospels. Our search is to discover if these are in harmony with his implicit claims. If they are, we certainly cannot say that he *could not have made* them. We will be more inclined to accept the Gospels at fact value.

(1) Matthew 11:25-27 is a famous passage in point. Jesus is alleged to have claimed that only the Father knew him, that he alone knew the Father, and that the knowledge of others must be mediated through him. K. A. von Hase described this saying as a "thunderbolt from the Johannine sky." [32] As suggested above, we cannot say that Jesus could not have made such claims. But did he? The authenticity of the passage has been attacked on two main grounds: that it is more Johannine than Matthean and that its form and content show it to be a Hellenistic "revelation word." [33] Hunter argues for the authenticity of the passage and concludes that it is a unique claim made by a unique person. [34] It has now been learned that the saying is not in the nature of "hellenistic revelation saying." [35] Rather it is semitic in character and shows itself to be of Palestinian origin. [36] It seems then that this saying, containing claims which the content of no title could surpass, must be judged authentic. Denial of its authenticity reveals bias rather than historical judgment.

(2) The term Messiah, is applied very seldom to Jesus in the Synoptics. The Gospel writers, even John, are very restrained in attributing a claim of messiahship to Jesus. In the Synoptics, only seven passages (eliminating parallels) indicate that Jesus used or accepted the title as applied to himself. Some of these are questionable, i.e., it is not certain that Jesus meant to apply the title to himself (Mark 9:41; 12:35; Matt. 23:10; 24:4). One is a postresurrection passage (Luke 24:26,46). Only two passages call for serious consideration: the confession at Caesarea-Philippi (Mark 8:29; cf. Matt. 16:16; Luke 9:20) and Jesus' answer to the high priest at his trial (Mark 14:62; Matt. 26:64; Luke 22:67). Even in John, Jesus is said to have applied the title to himself in only two passages (John 4:24-25; 17:3).

The report of the confession of Peter at Caesarea-Philippi is reported

[32] Die Geschichte Jesu, (Leipzig, 1876), p. 422.
[33] A. M. Hunter, "*Crux Criticorum*—Matthew 11:25-30—A Re-appraisal," NTS, 8, pp. 241-249.
[34] *Ibid.*, p. 245.
[35] *Contra.* Bultmann, *History of Synoptic Tradition.* p. 159.
[36] Jeremias, *Prayers*, p. 45.

differently in Mark (followed by Luke) and Matthew. In Mark, the confession is made, Jesus enjoins silence, and he begins immediately to interpret his ministry in terms of the Son of man. Though Jesus did not repudiate the title, he seems to have accepted it reluctantly. Matthew seems to have enlarged the account to include the Christian understanding of its true meaning. Peter is congratulated by Jesus and told that his understanding comes from the Father. This is followed by the saying about the building of the church and the keys of the kingdom.

While I am inclined to accept Mark's account as nearer to the historical facts, I would recognize that Matthew's account is a true interpretation. It *was* the Holy Spirit who revealed the truth about Jesus to Peter. It *was* the confession of Jesus as the Christ which laid the foundation for the erection of the church. But I rather doubt that Jesus said so at the time or that the disciples understood this at the time. It was made clear by subsequent events. Matthew's account is therefore true to the inner reality of the event.

The answer of Jesus to the high priest is also reported differently in the three Gospels. Matthew (26:64) quotes it as, "You have said so." Mark (14:62) has the unequivocal "I am." (Luke 22:67) has, "If I tell you, you will not believe." My inclination would be to accept Matthew's account as being nearer to the historical fact, mainly because it conforms to Mark's account of the confession. Jesus does not repudiate the title (he could have saved his life by doing so), but immediately (as all three agree) began speaking of the Son of man seated "at the right hand of Power."

If our analysis of these passages is correct, Jesus knew himself to be the Messiah but was unwilling to accept the Jewish content of the title.[37] While he did not repudiate the title, he accepted it reluctantly. He did not want it publicly attributed to him until events had changed the content and reshaped the concept.

(3) Only Jesus is said to have called himself the Son of man. It is used eighty times in the Gospels.[38] With one exception (Stephen's use in Acts 7:56), the full title is found nowhere else in the New Testament. Much has been written about this title and widespread differences exist. Modern scholarship has not arrived at any real understanding of it. It seems to me that the number of times Jesus

[37] See Moule's argument (*Phenomenon,* pp. 70-71) which reaches the same conclusion.
[38] Stauffer, *Jesus and His Story,* p. 133.

is said to have used it, its absence from the rest of the New Testament, and the fact that no one else ever called him "the Son of man" indicates a genuine remembrance of the earthly Jesus. He did use the title for himself. However, the content and meaning of the title as well as its background is so hopelessly obscure that we can derive little from it. The mere fact remains that Jesus did use it.

(4) Concerning the title, Son of God, or the absolute use of Son, little can be said with certainty. There is no doubt that Jesus exhibited a filial devotion to the Father that was unique. This is woven into the fabric of his ministry. The title, even if Jesus used it or accepted it, did not have the metaphysical content given it by Christian creeds. Rather, it described one who functioned as the Son of God, one who gave filial obedience, one whose ministry was the channel of God's action in the world. There can be little doubt that, in these ways, Jesus thought of himself as the Son of God.

In conclusion, we must content ourselves with seeing in the words and conduct of Jesus a self-understanding which conformed in *essential substance* to the titles ascribed to him after his resurrection. The *explicit* Christology of the early Christians was no more exalted than the implicit Christology of Jesus himself. To this extent, the tradition can be validated. It contains a true reminiscence of Jesus' own self-understanding. Thus, the reliability of the Gospels, the fact that they mediate the real Jesus to us, need no longer be doubted.

PART II
THE
TEACHINGS OF
JESUS

The main themes of Jesus' teaching could be included in one chapter, a chapter on the kingdom of God. However, we have chosen to treat them under three headings: kingdom, God, and discipleship. Since critical problems have been dealt with in Part I, we will pay little attention to them in this section of our study. We will try to avoid anachronisms. We will try to maintain the distinction between the time of Jesus and the time of the Christians. This is especially important in a discussion of discipleship.

CHAPTER VI
JESUS' PROCLAMATION OF THE KINGDOM OF GOD

Jesus often spoke of the kingdom of God. It has long been recognized that this was the central motif in his preaching. The kingdom, of which he spoke, had not always existed but is a reality which approaches (Mark 1:15), is near (Luke 21:31), comes (Luke 17:20-21), or arrives (Luke 11:20). Sometimes he seems to speak of it as future (Mark 9:1), sometimes as impending (Matt. 10:7), and sometimes as already present (Luke 11:20). He speaks of the Law and the Prophets as being until John the Baptist and the kingdom as being present since then (Matt. 11:16). Paradoxically, then, Jesus spoke of the kingdom as having already but not yet come.

The kingdom was hidden. It did not come "with signs to be observed" (Luke 17:20-21); it had to be announced (Luke 9:60) both by Jesus (Mark 1:15) and by his disciples (Luke 10:9). It was good news; he spoke of the "gospel of the kingdom" (Matt. 4:23; 9:35;

24:14) and is said to have "gospelized" it, i.e., announced it as good news (Luke 4:43; 8:1; 16:16).

The kingdom is an object of thought. Jesus could speak *about* it (Luke 9:11) and people could hear its word (message) either with or without understanding (Matt. 13:19-23). The "secret" (Mark 4:11) or "secrets" (Matt. 13:11; Luke 8:10) of the kingdom were a matter of intellectual apprehension, but also of spiritual understanding which came from God.

The kingdom is not mere doctrine, a matter of theology. It confronts men with the necessity of decision; it challenges them to repent (Mark 1:15). It is a sphere of life into which one may enter or from which one may be excluded (Matt. 5:20). While right doctrine does not bring one in, wrong understanding can shut one out of the kingdom (Matt. 23:23).

Entrance depends not on legalistic or religious works (Matt. 7:22-23) but on a decision to follow Jesus (Matt. 10:32-33). It is a gracious gift of God into which harlots and tax collectors (Matt. 21:31) and Gentiles (Matt. 8:11) enter while Jews who depend on their status or works are cast out (Matt. 8:12).

To be in the kingdom is life's greatest blessing. It is better to be maimed than to be excluded (Mark 9:47). Entrance is worth any sacrifice, even to that of becoming a voluntary eunuch (Matt 19:12). The rich find it difficult to enter (Mark 10:25-35), but it belongs to the poor (Luke 6:20; cf. Matt. 5:3). Those who enter must come as little children (Mark 10:15). Those who cry out for mercy are justified while those who boast of righteousness are rejected (Luke 18:9-14). Only those who give full allegiance to Jesus are "fit" for the kingdom (Luke 9:62). The disciples are to pray for its coming (Luke 11:2); they are to seek it first of all (Matt. 6:33), trusting God to provide the necessities of life.

Those who are in the kingdom are different from those outside. They have a new goal in life (Matt. 6:33); they love God with their whole being and their neighbor as themselves (Mark 12:29-31; and parallels). They are poor in spirit (Matt. 5:3). They mourn for their sins, hunger and thirst after righteousness, and are meek under the hand of God (Matt. 5:4-6). They express their allegiance to Christ in good works to their fellowmen (Matt. 25:34-46); greatness in the kingdom comes through service (Mark 10:42-45).

What did Jesus mean by the kingdom of God? Our modern word,

kingdom, is completely misleading. Rarely, if ever does the idea of territory or realm enter into its use in the New Testament.[1] Kingdom in Jewish and Greek usage had an active meaning. It spoke of God as ruling, of his power as expressed in deeds, of his activity as king.[2] It described the exercise of the sovereign power of God.[3] Kingship was not an "office but a function"; it was not a title but a deed.[4] To the Jew, it was above all a personal relation between a king and his subjects.[5]

Jesus did not explain what he meant by the kingdom of God; he did not need to. The term was common; it could easily be understood by his contemporaries. The thought of God as king constitutes one of the oldest strands of Old Testament thought. It provided an apt description of the relationship between God man: God as Lord demanded obedience and in return gives his people protection and help.[6] Two shades of meaning characterize Israel's thought of God as king. There are passages which stress the timelessness of God's kingship (cf. Ex. 15:18; 1 Sam. 12:12; Ps. 145:11) and there are passages which stress the expectation of the future reign of God.[7]

Later Judaism developed the idea of the kingdom of Heaven ("Heaven" was the pious Jew's substitute for "God.")[8] The term is found much more frequently in rabbinic literature than in the Old Testament. Three meanings are discernible: (1) The obedient Jew was said to have taken the "yoke of the kingdom" upon him, (2) The kingdom was spoken of as the nation of Israel, and (3) The kingdom was spoken of as coming in the future.[9]

This is not to say that Jesus simply took over the Jewish concept and used it without modification. He, as the Jews did not, connected the idea of the Messiah and the kingdom of God.[10] He neither confirmed nor renewed the national hopes of the Jews.[11] He never prom-

[1] J. Bonsirven, *Theology of the New Testament* (London: Burns & Oates, 1963), p. 37 and Jeremias, *Theology*, p. 98. However, S. Aalen (" 'Reign' and 'House' in the Kingdom of God in the Gospels," *NTS* 8, pp. 215-240) takes the opposite position.
[2] Perrin, *Rediscovering*, p. 55.
[3] C. H. Dodd, *The Parables of the Kingdom* (New York: Scribner's, 1961), p. 24.
[4] R. Schnackenberg, *God's Rule*, p. 13.
[5] T. W. Manson, *Ethics and the Gospel* (London: SCM, 1960), p. 28.
[6] G. van Rad, *TDNT*, V 1, p. 568.
[7] *Ibid.*, pp. 568-569.
[8] Kuhn, *TDNT*, p. 571.
[9] Bornkamm, *Jesus*, pp. 15,65 and Dodd, *Parables*, p. 23 and Kuhn, *TDNT*, pp. 572-573 and Perrin, *Kingdom*, p. 113.
[10] Kuhn, *TDNT*, V. 1, p. 574.
[11] Bornkamm, *Jesus*, p. 66.

ised the restoration of the kingdom to David.[12] Most of all, his thought was different from Jewish thought in that he spoke of the kingdom as already present in his own life and ministry.[13]

Jesus did not define the kingdom of God. His teaching was not in abstract terms and definitions but in concrete terms and illustrations. His primary tool of speaking about the kingdom was in parables, some (twelve in all) were explicitly "kingdom" parables, many were not. He made frequent use of metaphors and similes which help us to understand him. Any attempt to systematize the teaching of Jesus does violence to the material. His teaching, like that of the rabbis, was occasional rather than systematic. Our western minds demand systematization, but we must do it with caution.

A working definition of the kingdom of God as Jesus saw it might be: *The unmediated rule of God in the lives of men, voluntarily accepted.* By his proclamation of the kingdom of God, Jesus announced the arrival of the promised day of redemption, challenged men to repent, and announced the final consummation of redemption in the future. Before discussing these points in detail, it is necessary to digress and discuss two questions that scholarly debate has forced upon us.

The time of the kingdom is a subject of great controversy. Did Jesus think of the kingdom as already present; as dawning, breaking in, or about to come; or as something belonging to the future? Kümmel surveys the various views held and lists three.[14]

First, there is the view propounded by Albert Schweitzer and supported by many other scholars. This view held that Jesus adopted the apocalyptic Jewish interpretation of the kingdom and looked for an imminent end of the world. Others, while holding that the kingdom was future to Jesus, see him thinking of it as about to come. Others see it as something belonging to the remote future.

Second, there is the view espoused by C. H. Dodd and supported by many modern scholars. This view holds that nearly all, if not all, of the kingdom passages refer to a reality present in the lifetime of Jesus. They tend to eliminate futuristic eschatology entirely from the teaching of Jesus.

Third, others have eliminated or pushed to one side the question

---

[12] *Ibid.*
[13] *Ibid.* and Dodd, *Parables,* p. 23.
[14] *Promise and Fulfillment,* pp. 15-16. Compare with J. A. Baird, *The Justice of God in the Teaching of Jesus* (London: SCM, 1963), pp. 123-124.

of time in the teaching of Jesus. They insist that the interpreter must ignore all statements of time.

There are, however, an increasing number of scholars who seek a mediating position. They believe that it is not a question of either/or but of both/and.[15] Where shall we position ourselves among this array of opinions? First, let us notice that there are certainly evidences that Jesus spoke of the kingdom as a present reality in his own lifetime. This is true whether we think of it as actually present, dawning, or breaking in. His exorcisms were a sign that "the kingdom of God has come upon you" (Luke 11:20; Matt. 12:28). Thus the power of God was "released in effective conflict with evil." [16] The individual was already having an experience of the kingdom of God.[17] Jesus spoke of the kingdom as "in the midst of you" or "in you" (Luke 17:20-21). The translation is irrelevant in this connection; either translation indicates that the kingdom was present.[18] Still another passage looks back on John the Baptist as the last of the prophets and says that the kingdom existed since John (Matt. 11:12; cf. Luke 16:16).[19] Further Mark 2:19 points to the ministry of Jesus as the day of salvation.[20]

Other passages could be cited and other evidence adduced,[21] but this is sufficient to show that Jesus thought of the kingdom as a present reality in his own time. Though not all could see it, though it could not be observed except through eyes of faith, it was a reality present in the world.

There is also evidence that Jesus thought of the kingdom as future. Paradoxically, it was *already but not yet.* Kümmel [22] argues against Dodd [23] that *eggidsein,* the Greek verb used to announce the kingdom cannot mean that it has already arrived, but that it is near, in the future, when time is involved (cf. Mark 1:15; 3:2; Matt. 10:7; Luke 10:9, 11). The second petition of the Lord's Prayer, "Thy kingdom come," (Matt. 6:10) implies some sense of futurity in the kingdom concept. Mark 9:1 confirms that the kingdom is still in the future

[15] Perrin, *Kingdom,* pp. 79-80 and Baird, *Justice,* p. 24.
[16] Dodd, *Parables,* p. 35.
[17] Perrin, *Rediscovering,* p. 67.
[18] *Ibid.,* p. 74 and Kümmel, *Promise and Fulfillment,* pp. 35-36.
[19] Bornkamm, *Jesus,* p. 66 and Käsemann, *Essays,* p. 43.
[20] Jeremias, *The Parables of Jesus* (New York: Scribner's, Revised Ed., c. 1963), p. 117.
[21] Perrin (*Kingdom,* pp. 74-78) summarizes the evidence.
[22] *Promise,* p. 26.
[23] *Parables,* p. 29.

to Jesus and his followers in some sense.[24] In the institution of the Lord's Supper (Luke 22:18; cf. Mark 14:25; Matt. 26:29), Jesus speaks of the future messianic banquet in the kingdom of God. Many promises of Jesus look forward to a future reversal of the present order in which the first shall be last (Matt. 19:30), the hidden revealed (Matt. 10:26), and the lowly exalted (Matt. 18:4; cf. Luke 14:11; 18:14). It is as impossible to eliminate the futuristic from the teaching of Jesus as it is to eliminate the concept of a present kingdom. Both elements must be recognized as an integral part of Jesus' proclamation of the kingdom of God. But how shall we reconcile these divergent thoughts? Perhaps the best way is by an analogy.

Christian salvation has a beginning, an eschatalogical beginning in conversion. But it does not end there. It continues in the developing Christlikeness of the Christian during his earthly life. But it does not end there. It comes to its ultimate meaning in the resurrection of the Christian and his entrance into heaven.

Likewise the kingdom of God had its beginning in the person and work of Jesus. This was its true "eschatological" beginning. In him the kingdom was established (or inaugurated) and the basis of all future dealings of God with man was laid. But it did not end there. If it had, the study of the kingdom would have only an academic interest. The kingdom continues. As each individual believes and *voluntarily* comes under the rule of God, the kingdom becomes a reality in his life. But that is not all. The kingdom will come to its ultimate consummation and meaning at the return of Christ, the end of the world, and our entrance into heaven. Then, and only then, will the rule of God become a perfected reality even in the lives of his own people. Bornkamm rightly warns against separating the future and the present. The future is revealed by the present; the present is illuminated by the future.[25]

Thus it is not a question of *either* present *or* future; it is a question of *both* present *and* future. The beginning lies in the ministry of Jesus. It may seem small and insignificant to men, but in it lies "the ultimate victory of God." [26]

The relation of Jesus' message to Judaism is variously estimated. What is the relation between the kingdom of God as Jesus proclaimed

[24] Kümmel, *Promise,* p. 28.
[25] *Jesus,* p. 92. Cf. Bright, *Kingdom,* p. 222.
[26] Bright, *Kingdom,* p. 222.

it and the hopes of the Old Testament and Judaism? The answer can be found in two words—continuity and discontinuity.

The fact of *discontinuity* is evident in the saying about the new patch on the old garment and the new wine in the old wineskins (Mark 2:21-22 and parallels). Jesus did not come merely to patch up Judaism nor as a religious reformer.[27] He insisted that his preaching constituted a new departure, a new beginning. Every attempt to blend the new with the old is doomed to failure.[28]

The idea of *continuity* between the teaching of Jesus and the Old Testament is contained in his claim that he had come to *fulfil* it. Each Synoptic writer has one or more fulfilment saying—the time (Mark 1:15), the Scripture (Luke 4:21), the Law and the Prophets (Matt. 5:17), and "all righteousness" (Matt. 3:15). The idea of fulfilment, but not the term, is found in Jesus' answer to the disciples of John (Luke 7:22-23). John wanted to know if Jesus was the one or if he must look for another. In reply, in a free quotation of Isaiah 35:5-6 and 61:1, Jesus pointed to his own works as the fulfilment of the Old Testament.[29]

Thus we see that Jesus' ministry was a consummation, a coming to pass, of Old Testament promises and of the hopes of Judaism. *But it was far more than that.* It was a fulfilment, a creative filling full of those hopes. Though Jesus might be said to "embody the ideal of the Old Testament," he proclaimed a new and revolutionary religion of his own.[30]

We must distinguish between consummation and fulfilment. "Consummation" means to bring to full expression what is inherent in and included in the past. Thus a man is the consummation of the boy; the man was inherent in and included in the boy. All that has been added is growth and experience. Likewise, heaven is the consummation of conversion; heaven is inherent in and included in conversion.

But "fulfilment" is more than that, even though the terms are synonyms in English. It is a creative filling full of the past by the addition of something which is qualitatively new. The hopes and dreams of the pious Jew could never be realized along the lines of the law and the prophets, nor along the lines of political victory.

[27] Jeremias, *Parables,* p. 118 and Dodd, *Parables,* p. 43.
[28] A. M. Hunter, *Interpreting the Parables* (London: SCM, 1960), p. 43.
[29] Jeremias, *Parables,* pp. 115-116.
[30] Bonsirven, *Theology,* p. 36.

Something different had to be added. This God did by sending his own Son into the world to redeem it. Christianity may be called the Jewish-Christian heritage, but we must remember that it is not simply Judaism in a new and refashioned garb. It is something entirely new. Thus, we must say that it is Judaism plus the coming of Jesus which resulted in Christianity.

1. The Arrival of the Day of Redemption

By his proclamation of the kingdom of God, Jesus announced the arrival of the day of redemption. Remember that our definition of the kingdom is: *the rule of God in the lives of men, voluntarily accepted.* Before the rule of God thus conceived could be realized, redemption and forgiveness of sins is required. Sinful man cannot *voluntarily* accept God's rule in his life. To announce the presence of the kingdom of God was to announce at the same time the arrival of the day of redemption. Three themes are discernible in the teaching of Jesus at this point: (1) that this rule was inaugurated in his own person and work, (2) that it was a gift of God's grace, and (3) that it was for all men.

(1) The Kingdom of God, the day of redemption, was inaugurated in the person and work of Jesus of Nazareth. It has long been recognized by scholars that Jesus' proclamation of the kingdom of God combined instruction and self-interpretation in an indissoluble unity.[31] Origen said that his person and mission were to be identified with the kingdom, that he was the kingdom itself—*autobasileia.*[32] Fuchs says that Jesus "hides himself" behind his teaching on the kingdom as its "secret content."[33] Kümmel says that the meaning of Jesus' message does not lie in apocalyptic revelations but in the fact that "in Jesus the kingdom of God came into being and will be consummated."[34]

Do the teachings of Jesus confirm this opinion of the scholars? Did he really believe that he was the inaugurator of the kingdom of God? Yes! There are a number of sayings, using the past tense, in which Jesus points to the significance of his coming. They are filled with the sense of an eschatological mission. These might be called the great "I cames," corresponding to the "I ams" of John.[35]

[31] E. Jüngel, *Paulus und Jesus* (Tübingen: J. C. B. Mohr, 3rd revised version), p. 87.
[32] Bonsirven, *Theology,* p. 38.
[33] E. Fuchs, *"Bemerkungen zur Gleichnisauslegung,"* *TLZ,* 79 (1954), Cols. 345-348.
[34] *Promise,* pp. 154-155.
[35] Robinson, *Jesus and His Coming,* p. 63.

I came, Jesus says: "to cast fire upon the earth" (Luke 12:49), "not to bring peace but a sword" (Matt. 10:34; Luke 12:51), "to set a man against his father, and a daughter against her mother, and a daughter-in-law against her mother-in-law" (Matt. 10:35; cf. Luke 12:52), "to fulfil" the Law and the Prophets (Matt. 5:17), "not to call the righteous but sinners" (Mark 2:17), "to serve, and to give my life a ranson for many" (Mark 10:45), and "to seek and to save the lost" (Luke 19:10). In all of these sayings, Jesus emphasizes the decisive importance of his ministry for the destiny of men.[36]

That Jesus thought of his ministry as a turning point and a new departure is shown by his sayings about the foolishness of putting a new patch on an old garment or pouring new wine into old wineskins (Mark 2:21-22 and parallels).[37] The same thought is found in the answer of Jesus to the question, "Why do . . . your disciples not fast?" He said, "Can the wedding guests fast while the bridegroom is with them?" (Mark 2:18-19). The wedding was a symbol of the day of salvation in the language of the East.[38] Thus, Jesus was announcing that he himself was the bearer of redemption. Jesus also identified himself with Jonah as the "sign of the times" (Luke 11:29-32). This meant that he himself was the sign of God's working of redemption.[39] The saying in Luke 11:23: "He who is not with me is against me" also points to the eschatological significance of the person and ministry of Jesus.

The primary events in the ministry are also recorded to show the decisive importance of Jesus for the kingdom of God. The baptism and temptation experience show how fully his ministry was linked to the cross from the beginning. This is enforced by his predictions of his sufferings (Mark 8:31-32; 9:31; 10:33 and parallels). They point to the cross as the essential foundation of God's redemption and the forgiveness of sins. The triumphal entry into Jerusalem (Mark 11:1-10 and parallels) was an acted-out parable meant to proclaim the presence of the kingdom in Jesus, the Prince of Peace. Finally, the prayer of Jesus in Gethsemane (Mark 14:32-42 and parallels) shows a deep conviction on the part of Jesus that his ministry and death were

[36] Compare our discussion of the self-understanding of Jesus in the previous chapter.

[37] Perrin, *Rediscovering*, p. 81.

[38] Jeremias, *Parables*, p. 117.

[39] Luke's version is no doubt original. Matthew (12:38-42) translates the saying into Christian language and makes the resurrection of Jesus the sign. It was to Christians, but Jesus, himself, was in his own day.

essential to the accomplishment of the purpose of God. His plea, "If it be possible, let this cup pass from me" should be understood to mean, "If it be possible to save men any other way, let this cup pass from me."

Another element in the teaching of Jesus that shows his consciousness of the meaning of his ministry is that in which he sees himself as the fulfilment of Scripture. When he preached at Nazareth, he read from the book of Isaiah and said, "Today this scripture has been fulfilled in your hearing" (Luke 4:18-21, cf. Isa. 61:1). He did not mean that the drama of redemption would begin in the future but that it had *already begun* in his own person.[40] The answer of Jesus to John's question implies the same sense of the meaning of his ministry. John sent asking: "Are you he who is to come, or shall we look for another?" (Matt. 11:2). Jesus replied, "Go and tell John what you hear and see: the blind receive their sight and the lame walk, lepers are cleansed and the deaf hear, and the dead are raised up, and the poor have the good news preached to them. And blessed is he who takes no offense at me" (Matt. 11:4-6). He meant that his work was the fulfilment of the promises of the Old Testament. The kingdom of God had become a reality in him.[41]

The same consciousness of being the ultimate fulfilment of the Old Testament is seen in Jesus' testimony to John, the Baptist (Mark 2:13). John, you remember, had denied that he was Elijah (John 1:21), but Jesus gave him the title. Moule, with penetrating insight, has pointed out that John refused the title because it was tantamount to the title Messiah. Elijah, according to Malachi 4:5, precedes not the Messiah but the day of the Lord. Thus, Jesus was ascribing to John the Baptist the status of messiahship (as commonly conceived in his own day), but was reserving for himself a higher status. In essence he is saying that his coming is the coming of the "day of the Lord," a day of redemption as well as of judgment.[42]

The significance of the ministry of Jesus is shown also in the overthrow of Satan and his powers. The conquest of Satan was one of the benefits expected in the messianic age.[43] When accused of casting out demons by Beelzebub's power, Jesus replied: "No one can enter a strong man's house and plunder his goods, unless he first binds

[40] Bright, *Kingdom,* p. 201.
[41] Bornkamm, *Jesus,* p. 68 and Dodd, *Parables,* pp. 31-32.
[42] Moule, *Phenomenon,* pp. 71-72.
[43] Jeremias, *Parables,* pp. 122-123.

the strong man; then indeed he may plunder his house" (Mark 3:27). In reply to the same accusation, he said on another occasion: "If I by the finger of God am casting out demons; then has come the kingdom of God upon you." (Luke 11:20; cf. Matt. 12:28). Jeremias suggests that the "binding of the strong man" refers to Jesus' victory at the temptation experience.[44] Whether this is true or not, Jesus claimed that he had bound Satan and that his exorcisms were an experience of the kingdom of God.[45] The victory of God in Jesus' works did not result in the restoration of the land to Israel; it did result in the "restoration to wholeness of a single disordered individual." [46] Thus, Jesus saw in himself the defeat of Satan and the coming of God's rule in the world.

To this may be added the saying of Jesus that he saw Satan fall like lightning (Luke 10:18) and his assertion that a woman, bound by Satan for eighteen years, had been freed by his healing word (Luke 13:16). Jesus himself had entered the arena of conflict and won God's victory over Satan and his forces.[47] God's reign had already come and this was evident through his power to cast out demons.[48]

Thus we see that Jesus taught that the kingdom of God had come, that it was inaugurated in his own person and work.

(2) Jesus taught that the kingdom was a gift of a gracious God.

This means, first of all, that it is not something which man does or builds step by step; [49] It is something which God does. Jesus proclaimed that God was acting in a final and decisive way for the redemption of man.[50] He did not envision a long period of history in which God would bring about his purpose but believed that God was in his own life acting decisively.[51]

This thought that the kingdom is entirely the act of God is brought out most forcibly in the parable of the seed growing by itself, i.e., automatically (Mark 4:26-29). The activity of the farmer in plowing, planting, and cultivating is completely ignored. All he does is wait.[52] That is the point of the parable. Man can do nothing to bring in

[44] *Ibid.*
[45] Perrin, *Rediscovering,* p. 67.
[46] *Ibid.*
[47] Bornkamm, *Jesus,* p. 68.
[48] Bultmann, *Theology,* p. 7.
[49] Reumann, *Jesus,* p. 151.
[50] Perrin, *Rediscovering,* p. 57.
[51] Dodd, *Parables,* p. 169.
[52] Bornkamm, *Jesus,* p. 73.

the kingdom; he must wait for God to do it. Perhaps Jesus was warning men against trying to take matters into their own hands as the Zealots were trying to do.[53] Nor can man follow the program of the Pharisees and bring in the kingdom. Neither strict observance of the commandments nor penance could avail; only God could bring the kingdom to reality.[54] Perhaps Jesus was thinking of his own ministry as the planting and the final judgment as the harvest.[55] Jesus was saying that the apparently insignificant thing they saw in his ministry was actually the ushering in of the kingdom.[56] The beginning was in sharp contrast with the end, but contrast is not the whole truth of the parable. The thought is that the harvest is the result of the planting; the ultimate victory is guaranteed by the planting.[57] But the primary thought is that it is the power of God and that alone which accomplishes both the planting and the ultimate victory.

A like teaching is found in the twin parables of the mustard seed and the leaven (Matt. 13:31-33 and parallels). Again the contrast is between the beginning and the end. The natural process which transforms a tiny seed into a shrub is to be matched by the spiritual miracle through which God would transform the ministry of Jesus into his own rule in the lives of men.[58] The dynamic power of God in bringing the kingdom to realization is compared to the pervasive power of yeast when it is placed in dough.[59] In the ministry of Jesus, behind and beneath what men see, is the dynamic power of God bringing forth his kingdom.

Not only is the kingdom the work of God; it is also a work of grace. "Grace" means unmerited favor. It is the love of God "at work in Jesus Christ for the salvation of men." [60] Jesus is always careful to point out that man does not deserve the mercies of God. In the simile of the father and child (Matt. 7:9-11 and parallel), Jesus assumed it to be axiomatic that the earthly father was evil. Yet, he gives good gifts to his children. Arguing from the lesser to the greater,

[53] E. Wright and R. Fuller, *The Book of the Acts of God* (Garden City, New York: Doubleday, Anchor Books edition, 1960, first published in 1957), p. 269. Fuller wrote the New Testament portion and will be cited alone hereafter.
[54] Bultmann, *Theology*, p. 7.
[55] Dodd (*Parables*, p. 144), however, sees the planting as past event and Jesus' ministry as the harvest.
[56] Fuller, *Acts*, p. 269.
[57] Jeremias, *Parables*, pp. 152-153.
[58] Hunter, *Parables*, p. 44.
[59] *Ibid.*
[60] *Ibid.*, p. 54.

he proclaims that God will give "good things" to those who ask him.

The parable of the workers in the vineyard, or the good employer as Jeremias prefers,[61] points to the graciousness of God. Each worker receives an equal wage regardless of the number of hours worked. This is a picture of divine generosity, of "sheer compassion for the unemployed." [62] Even so, God gives without regard to the strict demands of justice.

Most beautiful and impressive among the parables that speak of God as seeking and saving the lost are the three parables in Luke 15.[63] Usually they are called the parables of the lost coin, the lost sheep, and the prodigal son. But they are really parables of the love of God who seeks the lost and disenfranchised and restores them to usefulness. The climax of the story is the elder brother. One can understand how God can love the returning prodigal; it is difficult to see how he could love the proud, haughty, and complaining brother. The parables describe with simplicity what God is like.[64] The parable of the two debtors (Luke 7:41-45) who loved in proportion to the debt forgiven also speaks of the forgiving love of God. The parable of the unmerciful servant (Matt. 18:23-25) who, though forgiven much, refused to forgive little, shows that the mercy of God is directed to the greatest of sinners.

In summary, it may be said that one of the most consistent strains in the teaching of Jesus is that the kingdom of God, the day of redemption, is God's act and it is an act of grace and love.

(3) In announcing the arrival of the day of redemption, the kingdom of God, Jesus proclaimed a salvation for all men.

Naturally, it was impossible for Jesus to announce salvation for the Gentiles during his lifetime. There may be a hint of a Christian mission to include the Gentiles in Jesus' reminder that it was only the widow of Zarephath who was ministered to by Elijah and that it was Naaman the Syrian whom Elisha healed (Luke 4:25-28). The saying that many would come from "the east and west" to sit in the kingdom while its sons would be cast out (Matt. 8:11-12) carries something of the same implication. The idea may also be included in the parable of the two sons (Matt. 21:28-31). One of them, the one who promised obedience but did not give it, certainly was meant

[61] *Parables,* p. 136.
[62] Dodd, *Parables,* pp. 94-95.
[63] Fuller, *Acts,* p. 269.
[64] Jeremias, *Parables,* p. 131.

to be a symbol of Israel. The other may have been meant to be a symbol of the Gentiles, but this is not certain. No, the mission to the Gentiles had to be inferred from other elements in the teaching and conduct of Jesus. Preeminently and rightly, it was inferred from Jesus' concern for the outcasts and disenfranchised of Israel. If such people could be included in God's grace, surely the Gentiles also were invited to enter it.

Imagine the people's shock when Jesus told the parable of the Pharisee and the tax collector (i.e., publican) (Luke 18:9-14). The Pharisee was the religious ideal of the Jew. He, if anyone, would certainly be acceptable to God. Others might strive for acceptance; he was sure to receive it. On the other hand, the tax collector was considered a traitor to Israel, a sinner before God. He was as certain of eternal condemnation as the Pharisee was of justification.

Yet, it was not so in the story. They both went up to the Temple to pray. The Pharisee, with self-satisfied smugness, announced his goodness and paraded his religious acts before God. We need not suppose he lied. He simply presented himself as one who had a right to bargain with God.[65] The publican dared not lift his eyes to heaven but kept beating on his breast and crying out: "God be merciful to me, the sinner" (v. 13, my translation).

Jesus said, "I tell you, this man (i.e., the publican) went down to his house justified rather than the other" (v. 14). What was he saying? He was saying that God welcomes the despairing, hopeless sinner and rejects the self-righteous.[66] It was in this way that Jesus taught the universality of God's forgiveness. He opened the possibility of salvation to men to whom the Jews would deny it.

Not only by his teaching, but also by his "parabolic" actions, Jesus proclaimed salvation for all.[67] He accepted the hospitality of outcasts (Luke 19:5), received them into his own house and ate with them (Luke 15:1-2), and even called one tax collector as his disciple (Mark 2:14). When criticized for his actions, Jesus replied: "Those who are well have no need of a physician, but those who are sick; I came not to call the righteous, but sinners" (Mark 2:17). He implied that the forgiveness of God reached even the disenfranchised of Israel.[68]

---

[65] Conzelmann, *Outline,* p. 119.
[66] Jeremias, *Parables,* p. 144.
[67] *Ibid.,* p. 229.
[68] *Ibid.,* p. 125.

Bornkamm [69] has also pointed out that the ministry of Jesus was directed to people on the "fringe of society," men who were marked as accursed by the Jews.

This does not mean that Jesus looked with romanticism on evil men or associated with them on the assumption that they were better than the so-called righteous. His characterization of the Pharisees as righteous was ironic; he did not think they really were. Self-righteousness, then as now, is self-delusion. It does mean that Jesus opened the doors of God's kingdom to all men. Potentially all could become kingdom citizens, all could be forgiven, all could be accepted by God.

But, as we shall see, this acceptance was not automatic; it demanded decision on the part of the man who would be accepted. God is not presented as one who is ready to overlook sin and forgive the sinner in his sin; he is pictured as the righteous father who forgives the sinner in order to make him righteous.

2. The Necessity of Decision

Jesus' proclamation of the kingdom confronted men with the necessity of decision.

If there is anything about Jesus' teaching on which scholars are agreed, it is that it was "crisis" teaching. His parables confront men with the necessity to decide about Jesus' own person and mission.[70] His proclamation of the kingdom of God called upon men to make a choice.[71] Bright has rightly said that Jesus did not come to impart a better and more spiritual ethical teaching nor to explain the character of God nor to correct the abuses of Jewish religious practice but to call men to a "radical decision" for the kingdom of God.[72]

According to Mark, Jesus' first message was: "The time is fulfilled, and the kingdom of God is at hand: repent, and believe the gospel" (Mark 1:15). This was a demand for a "complete reorientation" of man's life in God.[73] This fundamental call to decision is reenforced by a series of parables which are told in such a way that the hearer cannot be a spectator.[74] He must become involved; he must decide. In the parable of the sower (Mark 4:1-9), for instance, the hearer

[69] Jesus, p. 79.
[70] Jeremias, Parables, p. 230.
[71] R. Bultmann, Jesus and the Word (New York: Scribner's, 1945), p. 51 and Fuller, Acts, p. 267.
[72] Kingdom, pp. 223-224.
[73] Fuller, Acts, p. 267.
[74] Bornkamm, Jesus, p. 74.

is the soil on which the word falls. Its fate is his fate for time and eternity. No wonder Jesus said at the end, "He who has ears to hear, let him hear" (Mark 4:9). In the parable of the debtor (Matt. 5:25-26), the hearer is the debtor who does not have a leg to stand on before God. He is advised to settle his dispute at once; the time is the time for resolute action.[75] In the parable of the ten virgins (Matt. 25:1-12), the hearer is a foolish and unprepared virgin. He is reminded that now is the time for decision.

The parables of the net (Matt. 13:47-50) and of the tares (Matt. 13:24-30) speak of a gathering and a separation. The gathering is now taking place in the ministry of Jesus; the separation will take place at the end of time. But the separation is already contained in the gathering. They are two component parts of one action. The hearer sees himself as deciding now where he shall stand in the separation.[76]

The parable of the householder who lay sunk in sleep while the thief ransacked his house (Matt. 24:43-44 and parallels) warns that the time for sleeping is past. Men must wake up. They must repent. They must decide. The parable of the fig tree which bore no fruit (Luke 13:6-9) is given a year to prove itself. This means that the hearer must no longer trust his membership in Israel, but decide now to seek God's forgiving power.

The parable of the unjust steward, with all of its difficulties of interpretation, makes one thing clear (Luke 16:1-8). One must make preparation for the future judgment and *now* is the time to prepare. Here is a man in crisis. His virtue is that he acted decisively when faced with the crisis.[77] He had no illusions about the future and seized his last chance.[78]

These are only a few examples among many of the emphases of Jesus for his contemporaries (and for us). God's act in bringing in the day of redemption is reality. There is no excuse for any man to be lost. If he is lost, it is because he has rejected God and his agent of redemption, Jesus Christ. Each man must decide for himself and his decision for or against Jesus will determine his fate for all time.

[75] Jeremias, *Parables*, p. 180.
[76] Jüngel, *Paulus und Jesus*, p. 147.
[77] Perrin, *Rediscovering*, p. 115.
[78] Bornkamm, *Jesus*, pp. 87-88.

(1) The decision demanded to enter the kingdom is a radical decision.
Jesus often stressed the fact that he who would enter the kingdom
must be in dead earnest about it. His decision must be radical, involving the whole man and all his relationships. Jesus wished no rash
disciples who lightly decided and then drew back. He insisted that
the way which leads to life is hard and the gate narrow (Matt. 7:14;
Luke 12:24).[79]

Would-be disciples who wished first to be assured of security, or
to bury their dead, or to say farewell to their friends were told, "No
one who puts his hand to the plow and looks back is fit for the
kingdom of God" (Luke 9:57-62). Jesus meant that the response to
the kingdom demanded all; it must supersede all of life's other "re-
sponsibilities and duties." [80] Jesus insisted that anything that hinders
entrance into the kingdom must be eliminated even if this meant
cutting off one's hands or plucking out one's eyes (Mark 9:43-48).
He insisted that the man who came to him must be willing to renounce
his family and even his own life (Luke 14:26).

The saying about the return of the evil spirit with seven other spirits
more evil than himself into the house "empty, swept, and put in order"
(Matt. 12:43-45 and parallel) shows that mere moral reform is not
enough for entrance into the kingdom. Not only must there be an
emptying; there must also be a filling. Man must empty self of sin
and selfishness, but he must also receive and fill his heart with God.

The parable of the great supper (Matt. 22:1-10; Luke 14:15-24)
condemns the flippance of invited guests who excused themselves
from the final call. The story condemns the Jew who thinks that he
will automatically "sit at the table with Abraham, Isaac and Jacob
in the kingdom of God." He will not unless he responds to the
challenge of Jesus *now.*[81]

Jesus insisted that men count the cost of discipleship before making
their decision. The story of the builder who had to stop his building
with the foundation (Luke 14:28-30) and the king who must decide
if he has hope of victory before going to war (Luke 14:31-32) teaches
this lesson. "So therefore, whoever of you does not renounce all that
he has cannot be my disciple" (Luke 14:33). Jesus did not attempt

[79] Hunter, *Parables,* p. 65 and Perrin, *Rediscovering,* pp. 144-145.
[80] Perrin, *Rediscovering,* p. 144.
[81] *Ibid.,* p. 114.

to keep men from following him; he did call for complete commitment.

The earnestness and sincerity of Zacchaeus (Luke 19:1-10) illustrates the kind of decision demanded. The parable of the two sons (Matt. 21:28-32) shows that performance, not promise, is demanded. The scribe who approved Jesus' saying on the great commandment but who was then only "not far from the kingdom" (Mark 12:32-34) shows that decision, not understanding is demanded. The parables of the treasure (Matt. 13:44) and the pearl of great price (Matt. 13:45-46) show that our decision must involve a readiness to sacrifice all else for the kingdom.[82]

(2) To enter the kingdom one must recognize his own sinfulness and renounce any claim of merit before God. Jesus assumed that all men were sinful; this was axiomatic to him. He spoke to the crowd and said, "If ye then being evil" (Luke 11:13). Plainly he assumed that none was sinless. In discussing a recent catastrophe, he asked, "Do you think that these Galileans were worse sinners than all the other Galileans, because they suffered thus? I tell you, no; but unless you repent you will all likewise perish" (Luke 13:2-3). He spoke of all manner of evil that comes out of the evil heart (Matt. 15:18-20).[83] Certainly, it is implied that no one can enter the kingdom unless he recognizes and confesses his sinfulness.

The need for recognition of sinfulness comes out most clearly in the various passages where Jesus condemned and denounced self-righteousness. In the parable of the debtor (Matt. 5:25-26) the reason for seeking a settlement out of court is that the man does not have a leg to stand on in court. He who seeks to stand on his own merits before God will soon find that he has no merits on which to stand.

The husbandmen who refused to pay their rightful rent (Mark 12:1-9 and parallels) are a picture of the self-righteous Jews who claimed to serve God, but did not. Using their own Scripture quotations, Jesus denounced them as giving lip service to God while their hearts were far from him (Mark 7:6-8). They were like the brother who promised to obey his father but did not (Matt. 28:28-31). They were like the contemptuous guests who excused themselves from the king's banquet out of contempt for the king (Matt. 22:1-10). The street people, whom they despised, "both good and bad" (v. 10) were broguht into the

[82] Jeremias, *Parables,* p. 201.
[83] Conner, *Faith,* pp. 120-122.

feast while they were excluded. They were like the rich man who forgot the law while indulging himself in pleasurable living (Luke 16:19-21). Neither he, nor his brothers who were like him, would be saved from the fires of torment. Finally, he denounced them as petulant children playing in the marketplace (Matt. 11:16-18; Luke 7:31-35). They did not seek to please God but condemned both John and Jesus and this for opposite reasons.

In other strands of his teaching, Jesus insisted that men were acceptable before God only when they recognized and confessed their sins. The classic example of this is the publican (Luke 18:9-14) who continually confessed himself to be *the* sinner. He was accepted while the self-satisfied Pharisee was rejected. To the same end is the saying of Jesus that one must become as a little child to enter the kingdom (Matt. 18:4). The story of the prodigal son teaches that such a childlike spirit involves the confession of guilt (Luke 15:18). The one who would enter the kingdom and enjoy the blessing of forgiveness must see himself as a sinner before God. He must seek mercy, not justice. Only thus may he enter it.

(3) To enter the kingdom one must reorient his life in God. The response to God's gracious act is that kind of response which reorients one's whole life in God. God becomes the center of life; he takes over the house of life as his own abode.[84] The rule of God is the personal, spiritual rule of God in the hearts of men. It consists of a relationship, a new relationship to God. The content of the decision that puts God at the center of one's life is described by three expressions in the teaching of Jesus. These expressions point to the same reality but from a slightly different perspective.

a. *Man must repent.* Both John the Baptist and Jesus came calling men to repentance (Mark 1:14-15). Repentance became the favorite word of Jesus to describe man's response to the kingly rule of God. He upbraided the cities where his mighty works had been done because they had failed to repent and said that the same works would have produced repentance in Tyre and Sidon "long ago" (Matt. 11:20-21). He said that the men of Nineveh would condemn his contemporaries because "they repented at the preaching of Jonah" and his generation had not repented in the presence of something greater (Matt. 12:14; Luke 11:32). He sent the twelve out to preach that "men should repent" (Mark 6:12). He described his mission as calling "sinners·

---
[84] Hunter, *Parables,* p. 49.

to repent" (Luke 5:32). He proclaimed, "unless you repent you will all likewise perish" (Luke 13:3), and announced the joy in heaven over one sinner that repented (Luke 15:7). He implied that the reason the rich man was in hell and his brothers headed that way was because they had failed to repent (Luke 16:30). Finally, Luke records the Great Commission as preaching "repentance and forgiveness of sins" (Luke 24:47. This is equivalent to "make disciples" in Matt. 28:19).

What did Jesus mean by the term? For an answer, we must not look to the meaning of the Greek word which means fundamentally simply a change of mind. No doubt, this is why Paul used the word only rarely in his preaching; his audience would not have understood the content of the decision demanded. Rather, we must look to the prophetic preaching of the Old Testament where repentance became the primary demand of God. Here, we find that the fundamental meaning of repentance is a reorientation of life to Yahweh and his will; it is a turning to Israel's God with one's whole being. This essentially meant three things: a readiness to obey God's will, unconditional trust in him with a renunciation of all human help, and turning from everything ungodly.[85]

This meaning for repentance explains why Jesus used that word to describe the decision for entrance into the kingdom. He also used faith, but only in relation to miracles. His audience were Jews. To them "believe" was primarily if not exclusively an intellectual matter. It was to credit the truth of a statement. Thus, they felt that they had faith if they recited the Shema, "There is one God" (cf., Jas. 2:19).

The change demanded was not a mere change of opinion about the truth or untruth of a theological statement. It was a decision that reached into the inner core of man's being, a complete revolution of his disposition and attitude toward God. God is not content with superficial change; "he does not claim *something*, but *me*."[86] Repentance means that man discovers the priceless treasure of God's rule and *joyfully* sacrifices all that he has in order to receive it (Matt. 13:44-46).[87] It means that he stops having contempt for God and accepts his gracious invitation even if it entails personal sacrifice (Matt. 22:1-10). It means self-renunciation.[88]

[85] Würthwein, *TDNT*, V. 4, pp. 985-986.
[86] Conzelmann, *Outline*, p. 118.
[87] Betz, *Know*, pp. 41-42.
[88] Bornkamm, *Jesus*, p. 83.

The opposite of repentance is illustrated in the stories of the rich young ruler (Mark 10:17-22) and the rich fool (Luke 12:16-20). These stories illustrate both the necessity of absolute self-renunciation and the difficulty of overcoming the pull of earthly riches. Concern for earthly riches blinded these two men to the surpassing treasure of the rule of God and robbed them of that greater treasure.[89]

b. *Man must be converted.* Conversion in the spiritual sense is not a common word with Jesus, but the one outstanding example of the demand is so meaningful that we must not neglect it as an expression of the vital content of man's decision for God. "Truly, I say to you, unless you turn (i.e., are converted) and become like children, you will never enter the kingdom of heaven" (Matt. 18:3; cf. Mark 10:15; Luke 18:17).

What "becoming like children" means has often been debated. Many have taken childhood to be a figure of innocence, but this does not seem to fit the context. Jeremias relates it to the use of *abba* and thinks that it is learning to call God, Father, with "child-like confidence."[90] But it seems more likely that the emphasis is upon humility, the sense of dependence of the child.[91]

A clue might be found in the saying of Jesus about "babes" and the "wise and understanding" (Matt. 11:25; Luke 10:21). The "wise and understanding" refers to the learned scribes who felt that acceptance with God was a matter of works. They must take upon themselves the yoke of the kingdom which was equivalent to scrupulous observance of the law.[92] The "babes" would be those who claimed no merit but depended upon the fatherly concern of God.

This is one of the most memorable and pregnant sayings of Jesus.[93] It teaches that a man must turn away from all sense of self-sufficiency and seek God as one dependent on his mercy. Thus conversion is another term for repentance.

c. *Man must surrender himself to God.* This is but another way of saying that he must repent and be converted. However, the concept of total surrender is often stressed in the teaching of Jesus; it must be recognized as a real element in the content of one's decision for God. One who would enter the kingdom must break completely with

[89] *Ibid.,* p. 88 and Jeremias, *Parables,* p. 165 and Perrin, *Rediscovering,* p. 88.
[90] Jeremias, *Parables,* pp. 190-191.
[91] Bornkamm, *Jesus,* p. 84.
[92] Dodd, *Parables,* p. 27.
[93] Perrin, *Rediscovering,* p. 146.

his past, even, if necessary from his family (Luke 14:26). He must be willing to renounce earthly obligations and follow Jesus without reserve (Luke 9:57-61). He must be willing to take the yoke of Jesus upon himself (Matt. 11:29) and learn meekness (i.e., surrender to the rule of God) from him who said, "My food is to do the will of him who sent me" (John 4:34). He must found the house of life firmly upon the rock, i.e., submission to the will of God (Matt. 7:21-27). The parable of the unclean spirit (Matt. 12:43-45) teaches that though a man is delivered from an evil spirit, he cannot be safe until God becomes master of the house of his life.[94]

All that is meant by surrender to God may be summed up in the words of the first and greatest commandment: "You shall love the Lord your God with all your heart, and with all your soul, and with all your mind, and with all your strength" (Mark 12:30 and parallels).

Thus, no matter how one expresses it—by repentance, conversion, or surrender—the content of the decision is the same. To enter the kingdom one must acknowledge the rulership of God in his own life; he must open his whole self to God; he must make God his God in reality.

3. A Final Consummation of Redemption

By his proclamation of the kingdom, Jesus announced a final consummation of redemption.

Jesus did not speak often of the future. His main concern was with the announcement of salvation and the call to repentance. However, there are a number of passages in the tradition which, contrary to Dodd, must be assigned to the end-time. Perhaps we can approach the futuristic teaching of Jesus best by discussing four subjects commonly included in a discussion of eschatology.

(1) Jesus taught the parousia (the future coming) of the Son of man. Scholars are sharply divided over the question of Jesus' teaching concerning the parousia, i.e., his so-called second coming. J. A. T. Robinson [95] denies that any of the parousia sayings in the tradition are authentic. Robinson is willing to admit, however, that Jesus expected a future end of all things, a final judgment of man, but denies that he expected a future and second coming for himself. Perrin has criticized him for admitting that history is bounded by the final

---

[94] Hunter, *Parables,* p. 49.
[95] *Jesus and His Coming.*

judgment in the teaching of Jesus and still denying that Jesus expected his own return, an event necessary to it.[96]

Dodd has interpreted the parables of judgment and crisis in such a way as to virtually eliminate the future element.[97] He takes such parables as the faithful and unfaithful servants, the waiting servants, the thief at night, and the ten virgins as belonging to the current exhortation of the Christian churches.[98] If we judge Dodd's position wholly on his book, we must include him among those who deny that Jesus taught a future coming for himself.

There can be no doubt, however, that the tradition preserved sayings attributed to Jesus which speak of his second coming. Our argument in Chapters 4 and 5 indicates that the tradition has preserved the substance of the teaching of Jesus. It seems highly unlikely that Christians would invent an entirely new strand of teaching and ascribe it to Jesus. Rather, the fact that it is so widespread and fundamental in the tradition argues for Jesus as its first source. The Christian's derived their expectation from him.

The parable of the talents (Matt. 25:14-30; cf. Luke 19:11-17) speaks of men entrusted with their master's possessions at his departure, of a time of activity by his slaves, and of the return of the master to call for an accounting of their stewardship. The parable plainly warns disciples that their Lord will come again and demand an accounting of their lives.

Jesus spoke of the coming of the Son of man at a time when men did not expect it (Matt. 24:37-46; cf. Luke 17:22-37). The authenticity of this saying is supported by the inclusion of the statement that Jesus did not know the time of this future event (Matt. 24:36). As noted above, no Christian would have invented such a saying. The stories of the thief in the night (Luke 12:39-40) and the ten virgins (Matt. 25:1-14) teach a similar truth. The Lord is coming. The time of his coming is uncertain. Man must be prepared for it. Disciples must be faithful because of their expectation of it.

(2) Jesus taught the future judgment of all men. Scholars agree that this is a basic element in the teaching of Jesus. He spoke of the gathering from all nations before the judgment seat and the separation of the sheep from the goats (Matt. 25:31-46). He spoke of a day

[96] *Kingdom,* p. 141.
[97] *Parables,* pp. 122-140.
[98] *Ibid.,* p. 122.

of judgment when it would be more tolerable for the "land of Sodom and Gomorrah" than for the town that refused to listen to his disciples (Matt. 10:15; Luke 10:12). A similar threat is made against the cities where his mighty works were done (Matt. 11:20-24; Luke 10:13-14). He spoke of a scene before his Father when he would acknowledge or deny men on the basis of their acknowledgment or denial of him on earth (Matt. 10:32-33; Luke 12:8-9). He insisted that only those who endured to the end would finally be saved (Mark 13:13; Matt. 10:22).

The parables of the tares and the net (Matt. 13:24-30, 47-50) speak of a future separation of the good and the bad.[99] The final judgment is also taught in the warnings of Jesus addressed to various groups. All Israel is warned by the parable of the barren fig tree (Mark 11:12-14). The parable of the rich fool (Luke 12:16-20) is addressed to the rich in Israel. The saying about the false prophets (Matt. 7:15-20) is addressed to the Pharisees.[100]

There is nothing in the teaching of Jesus that attempts to draw a picture of the final judgment. He was content to include the *fact* of final judgment as an integral part of his teaching.

(3) Jesus taught that kingdom men would enjoy a blissful future. He did not draw a detailed picture of the future hope of kingdom men, i.e., those who repented at his proclamation. This is the way of the apocalyptist (cf. Rev. 21—22), but little, if any, of it is found in the teaching of Jesus. However, there is no doubt that he taught a future consummation of the kingdom and pointed to attendant blessings for those who entered in.

In the institution of the Lord's Supper, he spoke of the festal banquet in the kingdom of the Father which he would eat with his disciples (Luke 22:15-20 and parallels). He spoke of the "many" who would sit at table with "Abraham, Isaac, and Jacob" in the future kingdom (Matt. 8:11). He spoke of Lazarus as being in the bosom of Abraham (Luke 16:19-31). He spoke of the kingdom prepared for his own "from the foundation of the world" and of the righteous entering into eternal life (Matt. 25:34,46b).

He spoke of the reversal of the injustices of this life in the life to come where the first would be last (Matt. 19:30), the hidden would be revealed (Matt. 10:26), the lowly would be exalted (Matt. 18:4; cf. Luke 14:11; 18:14; Matt. 23:12), the hungry would be satisfied

---

[99] Perrin, *Kingdom,* p. 188 and Jüngel, *Paulus und Jesus,* pp. 146-147.
[100] Jeremias, *Parables,* pp. 122-125 and Perrin, *Kingdom,* p. 189.

and the weeping ones would laugh (Luke 6:21).[101] There can be no doubt, then, that Jesus envisioned a future consummation of the kingdom. For those who repented and became kingdom men, this future life would be one of blessedness, of fellowship with God, and of boundless joy.

(4) Jesus said little about the future of the unrepentant. His teaching contains no detailed portrayal of their sufferings. What he says is more suggestive than exhaustive. He did accept the common belief that the future would be one of torment and regret.

The rich man in the torment of flames is pictured as seeking surcease from his own suffering and then asking for a messenger to warn his brothers of the future (Luke 16:19-31). Jesus warned: "The sons of the kingdom (i.e., unrepentant Jews) will be thrown into outer darkness; there men will weep and gnash their teeth" (Matt. 8:12; Luke 13:28). The judge's message to the unrepentant in the judgment is: "Depart from me, you cursed, into the eternal fire prepared for the devil and his angels" (Matt. 25:41). It is further said that "they go away into eternal punishment" (Matt. 25:46). But in all of this, there is no systematic picture of "hell," no detailed discussion of punishments.[102]

To sum up, Jesus was much more concerned with preaching the kingdom of God and the forgiveness of sins in the present than he was with the future. He was more concerned with calling men to repentance and helping them order their lives aright in this world than he was in warning them of the torments of the coming life. Nevertheless, he taught that the present contained the future. The time would come when all would come to judgment at the consummation of the kingdom. Those who heard and acted on his message would be blessed. Those who rejected him would be punished. There is no way of escaping the fact that Jesus, in this, was taking up and reapplying the common beliefs of his time. The distinctive difference between his teaching and that of the Pharisees was the grounding of man's destiny in their decision about him. Nor can there be any doubt, that the Christians took up his teaching without essential change. Neither of these facts, however, mean that the teaching was not an integral part of Jesus' proclamation. I think we have shown that it was.

---

[101] Perrin, *Kingdom,* p. 188.
[102] Reumann, *Jesus,* p. 245.

CHAPTER VII
JESUS' TEACHING ABOUT GOD

Jesus was the crucible through which the Old Testament understanding of God was refined and made Christian. This statement means two things. *First,* it means that Jesus adopted the Jewish conception of God. In no other area of his teaching is he so much the son of "Abraham, Isaac, and Jacob." Rather than proclaiming a new doctrine of God, he sought to clarify who and what God really was.[1] He built upon the Old Testament;[2] he often made use of Old Testament conceptions and terminology.[3]

Second, it means that Jesus refined, corrected, and enlarged the Jewish conception of God so that it became the standard Christian doctrine. Paul began his thought of God with "God, the Father of our Lord Jesus Christ" (an expression found often in his writings, cf. 2 Cor. 1:3). His conception of God came from Jesus.

What has been said does not mean that Jesus did not make notable

[1] Conzelmann, *Outline,* p. 99.
[2] Conner, *Faith,* p. 96.
[3] W. G. Kümmel, *Die Theologie Des Neuen Testaments nach Seinen Hauptzeugen Jesus—Paulus—Johannes* (Göttingen: Vandenhoeck & Ruprecht, 1969), p. 35.

advances over the Old Testament in his understanding of God. Though startlingly familiar when compared to the Old Testament, his teaching was strikingly different when compared to his contemporaries. His conception of God was on a "specifically higher lever" than the Jewish conception.[4] It represented an "epoch-making advance" on the Old Testament.[5] The content of his teaching was fresh and novel.[6] He eliminated the imperfections of the Old Testament and brought its excellencies to completion.[7] Perhaps the contrast can best be seen in the way in which God was addressed in prayer.[8] Jesus himself addressed God with the "stark simplicity of Father" and taught his disciples to do the same. The Jew, on the contrary, was taught to say three times daily: "Lord God of Abraham, God of Jacob, God of Isaac! God Most High, Creator of heaven and earth! Our Shield and the Shield of our Fathers" (cf. IV Esdras 8:20-22).[9]

Jesus taught about God, but not in the way of the modern theologian. He did not systematize his teaching but brought it into sharp focus on the situation he faced.[10] There is no single chapter in the Gospels to which one might turn and say, "here is Jesus' doctrine of God." However, there is scarcely a chapter in the Gospels which does not speak to us of Jesus' conception of God. Sometimes it appears in lucid clearness as in Matthew 18:14, "So it is not the will of my Father who is in heaven that one of these little ones should perish." Sometimes it lies below the surface of what he says. For instance, when Peter rebuked him for saying he must die, Jesus replied, "Get behind me, Satan! For you are not on the side of God, but of men" (Mark 8:33). Nothing is said about God in this passage, but a world of things is implied. God is sacrificial and self-giving; anyone who avoids sacrifice does not think of things like God does. When he admonished the disciples, "Love your enemies and pray for those who persecute you, so that you may be sons of your Father who is in heaven" (Matt. 5:44), much is implied about the kind of God God is. It follows that we must be alert to implied as well as expressed concepts if we are to understand Jesus' thought about God.

Jesus taught not only in words but also in conduct. We learn of

[4] H. H. Wendt, *The Teaching of Jesus* (New York: Scribner's, 1899), p. 184.
[5] *Ibid.*, p. 209.
[6] Fuller, *Acts of God*, p. 271.
[7] Conner, *Faith*, p. 96.
[8] Bultmann, *Theology*, V. 1, p. 24.
[9] *Ibid.*
[10] Conzelmann, *Outline*, p. 100.

his conception of God from what he did and was, perhaps more so than from what he said.[11] He was himself the "revelation of God," "the self-utterance of God in history."[12] His own fellowship with God was impressively immediate and constant. His filial devotion was always apparent. His prayer life inspired his disciples, men who had been trained in the Jewish way of prayer from childhood, to ask him to teach them to pray (Luke 11:1). His life was the true embodiment of God; he was the "true living Word of God, the image, the expression of Deity."[13] His compassion for people revealed what God's love meant. His wrath against hypocrites was the divine reaction against all sin and falseness.[14]

This fact, more than his teaching, has led Christians to believe that Jesus revealed God as he really is. Other men bear the "image of God," but the image is distorted because of sin. He bore it with fidelity. While others may be like God, God is like him. John has preserved this thought in a saying attributed to Jesus. In the farewell address, Jesus said, "If you had known me, you would have known the Father also; henceforth you know him and have seen him." When Philip demanded to be shown the Father, Jesus replied, "Have I been with you so long, and yet you do not know me, Philip? He who has seen me has seen the Father?" (John 14:7-9).

1. The Presuppositions of Jesus' Teaching About God

There are many elements in the Old Testament conception of God which Jesus adopted but did not stress. He spoke from them as basic presuppositions which he shared with his audience. Often he clarified without changing the basic position of the Old Testament teaching.

(1) Jesus accepted the existence of God without question. Like the Jews, Jesus took the existence of God for granted. He shared the Jewish belief that only the fool could say "there is no God" (Ps. 14:1) and that even demons "believe—and shudder" (Jas. 2:19).[14a] Jesus experienced God as a living reality. He knew him in direct relation. It would have been unthinkable to him that the existence of God needed to be either stated or proved. He would sooner have doubted his own existence than that of God.

---

[11] G. B. Stevens, *The Teaching of Jesus* (New York: Macmillan, 1902), p. 79.
[12] *Ibid.*
[13] *Ibid.*
[14] Conner, *Faith*, p. 105.
[14a] S. M. Gilmour, *The Gospel Jesus Preached* (Philadelphia: Westminster, 1957), p. 123.

(2) Jesus believed that God was personal; relationship with God was an I/Thou relation rather than an I/it relation. When he addressed God in prayer, he said, "I thank *thee,* Father, that *thou* hast *hidden* these things from the wise and *revealed* them to babes; yes, Father, for such was thy gracious *will"* (Matt. 11:25-26, italics mine). The italicized words in this quotation make it quite clear that Jesus thought of God as a personal being in some sense of the word. He addressed God with the personal pronoun, ascribed actions to him which are possible only to persons, and thought of him as making choices based on his will. One theologian has made intelligence, moral sensibility, and will the essential powers of personal life.[15] Jesus certainly ascribed such powers to God. Bultmann is right in saying that Jesus did not regard God as "metaphysical entity," "cosmic power," or "natural law." [15a] Jesus seemed never to be bothered by the objections that some modern theologians make to regarding God as personal; he simply accepted it as axiomatic that God was a person. His own personal and immediate relation to God made it impossible for him to think otherwise.

(3) Jesus assumed the transcendence of God. That God was acting in the world while not a part of it is everywhere assumed in the teaching of Jesus. In *this sense* Jesus shared the Jewish conception of the remoteness of God.[16] God was never confused with nature in his thought nor made a part of the world after the manner of pantheism. The doctrine of creation (Mark 13:19) meant, for one thing, that God was not contained in the world. The creation belief, in biblical thought, is not meant to explain how the universe came into existence; it is meant to explain the nature of the universe. The universe is relative, creaturely, a means to an end, not an end in itself. The Creator, on the other hand, is absolute. Thus, in the thought of Jesus, God was distinct from the world in which we live.

On the other hand, he was never thought of as separated from it nor as a stranger in it. He was the Lord of heaven and earth (Matt. 11:25). Heaven was his throne and earth his footstool (Matt. 5:34-35). It is God who determines the limits of human life; he says to the rich fool, "This night your soul is required of you" (Luke 12:20). He alone has the power to destroy both soul and body in hell (Matt. 10:28). All things are possible to God, even the salvation of a rich

[15] Conner, *Faith,* pp. 93-94.
[15a] *Jesus,* p. 151.
[16] Bultmann, *Jesus,* p. 150.

man (Mark 10:27). Jesus was confident that God could send twelve legions of angels to rescue him from the cross if he asked it (Matt. 26:53). Jesus condemned the Sadducees of not knowing the unlimited power of God because they doubted the resurrection; they did not know that God could create new forms of life which men could not conceive of (Mark 12:24).[17]

God is so transcendent that he is hidden from men in a mystery which can be penetrated only when God chooses to reveal himself (Matt. 11:27). God is never to be questioned or tested; he is to be trusted (Matt. 4:7). He governs the world and human life in their totality and alone knows the hour and day of the coming of the Son of man (Mark 13:32). His knowledge reaches to the hidden things of men (Luke 12:2) and penetrates the inmost thoughts of men's hearts (Luke 16:15).

Only he is to be worshiped (Matt. 4:10) and "Father" in a religious sense is to be reserved for him (Matt. 23:9). Man must love God with his whole being (Mark 12:29-30); religious devotion cannot be divided between God and mammon (Luke 16:13). Even in his teaching that men may address God as "Father" (Luke 11:2) there is no invitation to familiarity. God is not to be thought of as a democratic God. Matthew's version of the address of the Lord's Prayer (Matt. 6:9)—"Our Father who art in heaven"—whether or not it goes back to Jesus, is a correct interpretation of the thought of Jesus.

The transcendence of God meant, for one thing, his universality. He is the God of all men; his love is not restricted to the Jews nor to the pious among the Jews. Jesus taught the universality of God. Using Old Testament references to the widow of Zarephath and to Naaman the Samaritan leper, he implied that God blessed people of all nations (Luke 4:25-28).

(4) Jesus assumed that God was righteous, that his actions were motivated by ethical and moral considerations. God was not mere power. To the pagans, God was power; religion was an attempt to influence that power, to enlist it in man's service, to make God available to the worshiper. Jesus completely renounced such a notion of God even though we often find paganistic talk of God in some Christian circles today. (This is especially true when some Christians

---

[17] Wendt, *Teaching,* pp. 201-202.

talk about prayer and the practice of spiritual enthusiasts who claim to "have" the Holy Spirit.)

Jesus thought of God as the only one who deserved to be called "good" (Mark 10:17). This meant for one thing that God was unalterably opposed to evil, that he would destroy it. The coming of the kingdom was to be a day of joy to some, but a day of gloom to others. God could not minimize evil nor tolerate it; there could be no truce, here or hereafter, between God and evil.[18] Men who honored God with their lips but not with their hearts were soundly rebuked by Jesus (Matt. 15:5-9). Not those who simply say, "Lord, Lord," would enter the kingdom but those who make a practice of doing God's will (Matt. 7:21).

Sonship to God does not depend on physical descent but obedience (Mark 3:35). It is by good works that God's true glory is manifested (Matt. 5:16). Even the disciple could not presume on God. If he wished to be forgiven he must forgive (Matt. 6:14-15). If he wished to have his life recognized as good, he must perform the weightier matters—justice and love—as well as the lesser matters of the law such as tithing (Luke 11:42). One could not say that he truly loved God unless he also loved his neighbor as himself (Mark 12:28-31). Thus, we see that Jesus' conception of man's relation to God was controlled by his thought of God. Because God was good, religious relationship between men and God had to be "entirely moral." [19]

(5) Jesus assumed that God is sovereign over nature. This idea was basic in Judaism and often came to expression in the teaching of Jesus. With the Jews, Jesus believed that God was the creator of the universe (Mark 10:6-9; 13:19); contrary to them, he did not believe that God had ceased from his labor but that he was active in the world. He looked on his own miracles—casting out demons, healing the diseased, stilling the storm, and raising the dead—as the works of God (Matt. 12:28).

The things that we ascribe to the forces of nature Jesus ascribed to the minute control of God over nature. It is God that sends the rain and the sunshine (Matt. 5:45). It is he who clothes the grass of the field (Matt. 6:30) and feeds the improvident birds of heaven (Matt. 6:26). All these spoke to Jesus of the presence of God.[20] The

---

[18] H. Branscomb, *The Teachings of Jesus* (New York: Abingdon-Cokesbury, 1931), pp. 151-153.

[19] Wendt, *Teaching,* p. 209.

[20] Bornkamm, *Jesus,* pp. 119-120 and Bultmann, *Theology,* p. 23.

fatherly care of God is such that worry is senseless and wicked (Matt. 6:26-30). Perhaps, after all, the insurance company which calls a storm an "act of God" is closer to the truth than the meteorologist who calls it a "freak of nature."

To Jesus the forces or laws of nature were simply the normal control of God over the world in which we live. God was not removed from direct contact with men and the world. There was no need in his thought of God for fiery archangels, patron saints, mediators, or intercessors.[21] How different was the attitude of Jesus toward nature from ours! All too often we have put science in the place of God, made the so-called laws of nature absolute, and dispensed with any need for God in our thought of the world. We need to return to reality. There is no conflict between belief in God as the controlling power of nature and belief in science as the discipline that seeks to understand the normal working of this force. Science can never tell us what kind of force controls nature; it can only tell us how that force normally controls it. Faith alone can tell us the nature of that force. If we follow Jesus, we say it is God.

(6) Jesus assumed that God was sovereign over history. He has been accused of dehistorizing the notion of God, but Fuller is right in saying that Jesus was not solely concerned with the individual and his experiences.[22] God was the God of Abraham, Isaac, and Jacob (Mark 2:26, etc.); he was the God of David (Mark 2:25). He had sent the prophets to Israel throughout her history (Mark 12:1-9) and had led his people out of Egypt and given them the law. His control of history was such that he had "shortened the days" of the coming tribulation for the sake of the elect (Mark 12:20). Admittedly, Jesus did not emphasize this aspect of God's activity; he did not need to; it was axiomatic among those to whom he spoke. However, there is little doubt that he thought of God's control of history as complete.

(7) Jesus assumed that God is a righteous judge. Every man owes him an accounting.[23] God is to be feared as the one who can destroy both soul and body in hell (Matt. 10:38). Those who rejected Jesus would be denied at the last judgment; those who accepted him would be confessed (Matt. 10:32-33), but all must stand before the Father's tribunal. This included cities of the past such as "Sodom and Gomor-

---

[21] Branscomb, *Teachings,* p. 149.
[22] *Acts of God,* p. 271.
[23] Bultmann, *Theology,* p. 24.

rah" as well as cities of the present like those which rejected the message of the disciples (Matt. 10:15). It included Gentile cities like Tyre and Sidon as well as Jewish cities like Capernaum (Matt. 11:21-24).

The judgments of God, said Jesus, are righteous. The hypocrites who "devour widows' houses and for a pretense make long prayers" will "receive the greater condemnation" (Mark 12:40). Those who practice their religion to be seen of men will receive no reward (Matt. 6:1). The man who exalts himself will be humbled and the man who humbles himself (under the hand of God) will be exalted (Luke 14:11). All evildoers will be thrown into the furnace where men weep and gnash their teeth, but the righteous "will shine like the sun in the kingdom of their Father" (Matt. 13:42-43). Both the Beatitudes (Matt. 5:1-10) and the woes (Luke 6:24-26) teach the fact of ultimate reward or retribution.

This conception of God as the righteous judge was not central in Jesus' thought of God, but it is present in his teaching. Jesus did not replace the picture of a righteous judge with that of a kindly father; he does not exclude the idea of judgment.[24] Rather the heavenly Father is also the righteous judge. The fatherhood of God is conceived of in moral terms. His chief concern for his children is not that they should be happy but that they should be holy. "If we refuse to be holy, he loves us too well to let us be happy."[25]

2. Primary Emphases of Jesus in His Teaching About God

We turn now to what was central in the teaching of Jesus, teachings about God which received the primary emphasis. Even here, Jesus was not an innovator; he was a true child of Israel. Israel shared his beliefs, but some of them were so neglected, so marginal in Judaism, that they made little impression. It became necessary to shift the center of gravity from the transcendence of God (without denying it) to his imminence, love, and fatherly concern.

(1) Jesus emphasized the nearness of God. Contemporary Judaism had overemphasized the transcendence of God. In Jewish thought, God had been pushed further and further away from any direct contact with man. If God intervened in history at all, it was through angels,

[24] Conzelmann, *Outline*, p. 100.
[25] Conner, *Faith*, p. 103.

his Spirit, or his Word.[26] His remoteness from human life was emphasized in many ways. He was described by such terms as "heaven," magnificance," "Majesty," or "Glory." The use of his name was avoided whenever possible; his action was spoken of with a "divine passive" (i.e., "It was determined," not, "God has determined").[27] God had been pushed so far into the distance that his action in the present was barely discernible.[28]

Jesus changed all of this. Through his teaching that the kingdom of God was breaking in, he struck a new note of the immediate presence of God.[29] Men were made to confront God as a present reality.[30] His disciples were taught that God could hear and see what they said and did in secret (Matt. 6:4,6,18). They had no need to "heap up empty phrases" in their praying for "your Father knows what you need before you ask him" (Matt. 6:8). God watched over and approved the sacrificial gifts of his people (Mark 12:40-41). He revealed the true meaning of Jesus to Peter (Matt. 16:17) and the secrets of the kingdom to all the disciples (Matt. 13:17). To Jesus, God was near, a living reality in man's life.

(2) Jesus stressed the redemptive love of God. Though we have discussed this thought in our treatment of the kingdom of God, we need to remind ourselves of the degree to which it was central and characteristic in Jesus' teaching about God. The thought of God's mercy is at the heart of the Christian conception of God which finds its basis in the teaching of Jesus.[31] Jesus emphasized that God's goodness is active love. God is not pictured, as in some religions, as passive, needing nothing and wanting nothing. His love is active love seeking the good of men, not only in a general way, but manifested in his concern for the individual.[32]

This comes out, first of all, in the passages where God is pictured as self-giving and forgiving. Peter is rebuked and called Satan when he seeks to persuade Jesus not to go to the cross. His attitude was that of self-seeking humanity, not that of self-giving divinity (Mark 8:33). The will of the Father is for the salvation of all; he does not wish "one of these little ones" to perish (Matt. 18:14). God forgives

[26] Fuller, *Acts of God,* pp. 271-272.
[27] Bultmann, *Jesus,* p. 139.
[28] Bultmann, *Theology,* p. 23.
[29] Fuller, *Acts of God,* p. 272.
[30] Conzelmann, *Outline,* p. 100.
[31] Conner, *Faith,* p. 103.
[32] Branscomb, *Teachings,* pp. 154-155.

the greatest of sinners; Jesus proclaimed not only a hope of future forgiveness, but forgiveness as a present reality.[33] The penitent publican would be justified while the self-righteous Pharisee would not (Luke 18:9-14). The woman of the streets had experienced the reality of forgiveness and expressed her gratitude in humble debasement of self (Luke 7:36-50). The three parables of the love of the Father (Luke 15) speak of his concern over the lost.

The redemptive love of God is reflected in the action of Jesus as he companies with sinners and tax collectors (Mark 2:15-17). The disciple who would wish to prove himself the true son of his heavenly Father must love his enemies, pray for his persecutors, do good to those who hate him, bless those who curse him, turn the other cheek to him who strikes him, go the second mile with him who forces him to go one, and deny not his coat to him who would take his cloak (Matt. 5:44-45; Luke 6:29-35). It is only by showing mercy that one becomes like his heavenly Father who is perfect in this as in all other respects (Luke 6:36; Matt. 5:48).

The redemptive love of God is also shown in his provision for the good of men. He made the Sabbath for the good of men. (Mark 2:27). The Bible was his word to men (Mark 7:13). The Temple was the house of God meant to be a "house of prayer for all nations" (Mark 11:17; cf. Luke 6:4). Not only the institutions of the Old Testament but the redemptive action of the New finds its source in God. He is the Lord of the harvest to whom we should pray to send forth laborers into the harvest (Matt. 9:37-38; Luke 10:2). When the harvest comes, we are not to forget that it is *his* harvest (Luke 10:2). God is the lord of his servants and has determined who will be honored by sitting at the right hand and the left hand of Jesus in the future kingdom (Mark 10:40; Matt. 20:23).

Preeminently, the redemptive love of God is manifested in the ministry of Jesus himself. It was by the Spirit of God that Jesus cast out demons and freed captive spirits from the control of Satan (Matt. 12:28; cf. Luke 11:20). To one such liberated spirit who wished to accompany him, Jesus said, "Return to your home, and declare how much God has done for you" (Luke 8:39). The Samaritan leper who returned from his healing to thank Jesus is said to have been praising God (Luke 17:18). Jesus thought of his own career as having been predetermined by God (Luke 22:22) and faced the cross without

---

[33] Kümmel, *Theologie,* p. 39.

flinching because he thought it was God's will for him, the way through which God would bring salvation to men (Mark 14:32-42). Even the authority which the risen Christ was to exercise came from God; "all authority in heaven and earth has been given me," he said (Matt. 28:18).

In all of these ways, Jesus stressed in his teaching that God is a God of redemptive love. There is hardly another element in his teaching that is more central than this. As we turn to discuss the fatherhood of God, we must remain aware that this title, in Jesus' mind, was simply a special application of God's character as redemptive love.

(3) Jesus taught the fatherhood of God. Jesus was certainly not the first to think of God as Father. However, his treatment of the idea is highly original. It surpassed all that had gone before it and introduced elements into the idea which were completely new.

Even the Greeks had a conception of God as Father. In their mythology, Zeus was looked upon as the father-god from whom all other gods had descended. The Stoics (though essentially pantheists) thought of God as the father of the universe, of men as his children, and of his care for them as assured.[34] However, to the Greeks, looking on God as Father referred primarily to the origin of things and people and tended to degenerate into a pantheistic conception of God and the world.[35]

In Judaism and Christianity, however, the term does not refer to God as the cause of our existence; it refers to him as Father in the sense that he is responsible for the welfare of his children.[36] Israel thought of itself as the adopted children of God, chosen by him, and confirmed as his children by their deliverance from Egypt. Since they looked upon a historical event as the basis of their relation, the thought was never one of creation.[37] Thus, the Old Testament can speak of God as Father of the chosen people (Deut. 14:1), or of Israel as a whole (Jer. 30:9). Men could address God as Father in their prayers (Ps. 89:26) and the leaders of Israel, the kings, were called the sons of God (Ps. 2:6,7). But always, the fatherhood of God carried with it the necessity of obedience to God on the part of Israel.[38]

[34] Bornkamm, *Jesus,* p. 124.
[35] T. W. Manson, *The Teaching of Jesus* (Cambridge University Press, 2nd. ed., 1945), p. 91.
[36] *Ibid.,* p. 90.
[37] *Ibid.,* p. 91.
[38] Wendt, *Teaching,* p. 187.

We must remember however that this thought of God as Father was by no means the central or customary way of speaking of God.[39]

The Old Testament conception of God as Father developed to some extent in the rabbinic period. While there were still those who thought of all Israel as the sons of God, the dominant thought came to be that of an ethical relationship. God came to be thought of as the Father of the righteous rather than of the nation as a whole.[40] This restriction of the thought, though it narrowed the idea, laid the groundwork for "a greater universality."[41] Such passages as Wisdom 2:16; 14:3; Ecclesiasticus 23:1; Tobit 13:4 and 2 Maccabees 5:7 show that the thought has shifted from collective to individual piety.[42] However the national dimension always remained.[43]

We see that the concept of God as Father was not new with Jesus, but the way in which it was presented was new.[44] *In the first place,* it was new because of the term which Jesus used—the Aramaic word, *Abba* (Mark 14:36). This term was not a religious one; it belonged to family life. It represents the chatter of the Jewish child who addressed his father with *Abba;* it corresponds to our term, "daddy."[45] The use of this term *to address God* was unheard of in Judaism. It would have shocked the pious Jew as being too familiar and irreverent.[46] The term was undoubtedly original with Jesus; it has been impossible to find any Jewish parallels to its use.[47] The mere fact that the term survived in the Greek-speaking churches in its Aramaic form (Rom. 8:15; Gal. 4:6) shows that it was a part of the oldest tradition of Jesus' words.

Though Jesus extended the privilege of calling God, Father, to his disciples, he preserved a unique use of the term for himself. Many times we find Jesus saying, "My Father" or "thy Father" or "your Father." Never do we find him saying, "our Father." He never joined himself to his disciples in calling God, Father. His relationship with God was unique; it is always prior to that of others.[48] Conzelmann vainly challenges the evidence for this assertion and thinks it comes

[39] *Ibid.*
[40] Manson, *Teaching,* p. 92.
[41] *Ibid.*
[42] Conzelmann, *Outline,* p. 101.
[43] Bornkamm, *Jesus,* pp. 125-126.
[44] *Ibid.,* p. 100.
[45] Jeremias, *Prayers,* p. 109.
[46] *Ibid.,* p. 62 and Kümmel, *Theologie,* p. 36 and Bornkamm, *Jesus,* p. 128.
[47] Jeremias, *Prayers,* p. 109.
[48] Fuller, *Acts of God,* p. 272 and Bornkamm, *Jesus,* p. 128 and Jeremias, *Prayers,* p. 62.

from the thought of the community.[49] He fails to show how, if that
is so, the distinction arose and was maintained in the tradition. Bornkamm is right in saying that this distinction undoubtedly goes back
to Jesus himself.[50]

In the second place, Jesus was the first to make the idea of the
fatherhood of God the controlling factor in his thought about God.[51]
It was not central in Judaism, as we have seen. But it belongs to
the bedrock of Jesus' teachings; it permeates his whole thought about
God. The word has become so central in Christianity that Christianity
would no longer be itself without it.[52] The "clearness, certainty, and
fulness" of the doctrine is unique with Jesus.[53]

But is this centrality due to the use of Jesus or to the writings
of Matthew, Paul, and John? T. W. Manson [54] analyzes the various
uses found in the Gospels and the writings of Paul. He finds that
the evidence suggests that Jesus did not speak of the fatherhood of
God often or publicly but only occasionally to his closest friends and
followers. He thinks that the centrality of the teaching in the New
Testament is due to the use made of it in Paul, John, and Matthew.
However, he sees this, and rightly, as an attempt on their part to
bring out what was truly central in the gospel and the teaching of
Jesus. They only shouted from the housetops what had been "whis-
pered in the ear" in the more primitive traditions.

In the third place, Jesus was the first to extend the thought of God
as Father to the individual worshiper. He was the first to see the
Father-Son relation as essentially and exclusively personal and spiritual. On the one hand, the Old Testament never conceives of one
as a son of God apart from his membership in the nation; on the
other hand, Jesus never applies the Father-Son concept to the nation.[55]
To Jesus, the relationship was personal and direct. It did not depend
on one's inclusion in a "nation, institution, or organization." [56] God
treats men as persons. "Each man knows God . . . as a person, not
as an impersonal or semi-personal entity in an organization or institu-

[49] *Outline,* pp. 101-105.
[50] *Jesus,* pp. 128-129.
[51] Conner, *Faith,* p. 96.
[52] James Moffatt, *The Theology of the Gospels* (London: Duckworth, ca. 1912), p. 99.
[53] Wendt, *Teaching,* p. 209.
[54] *Teaching,* pp. 94-102.
[55] Conner, *Faith,* p. 97 and Bornkamm, *Jesus,* p. 126.
[56] Conner, *Faith,* p. 98.

tion in which the personal life is obscured if not destroyed." [57] If we would follow Jesus' thought, the fatherhood of God must never become a theological commonplace.[58] It must remain a dynamic reality of experience. This was what it was for Jesus. The thought of God as Father dominates "the whole ministry of Jesus from the Baptism to the Crucifixion." [59]

In the fourth place, the originality of Jesus is seen in that he extended the privilege of sonship to *all men.* Whether or not Jesus taught the universal fatherhood of God has long been a subject of intense debate. As is usual in debates of this kind, the problem is primarily one of semantics. It is certainly true that the love of God is universal. It does not manifest itself only to a single individual or group but is directed toward all men. If by fatherhood one means that God loves all men, there is no doubt that Jesus taught the universal fatherhood of God.[60] The right question seems rather to be, did Jesus teach the universal sonship of men? To this, a negative answer must be given. Not all men are sons of God; they have repudiated God and are not worthy of his name. Men must *become* the sons of God.[61] Nevertheless, it is true that Jesus extended the privilege of becoming the sons of God to all men. We might say that all men are *potentially* the sons of God, but only those who accept the role of sonship, who practice obedience, are *actually* sons of God.

What the fatherhood of God means in this special Father-Son relation can be illustrated by noticing two emphases of Jesus. *First,* he taught that God protects and cares for his children. He taught the disciples to be without fear in the face of one who could only destroy their bodies. The sparrow, he said, is practically worthless, yet not one falls to the ground "without your Father's will." "You," he added, "are of more value than many sparrows. Even the hairs of your head are all numbered" (Matt. 10:29-30; Luke 12:6-7). For a son of God, worry about the ordinary needs of life is both senseless and wicked. The Father clothes the grass of the field in splendor and feeds the improvident birds of the air. Surely he will care for us. To doubt this and make these things primary in life is to put ourselves in the class of men of the world. We are to seek God's

[57] *Ibid.*
[58] Manson, *Teaching,* p. 101.
[59] *Ibid.,* p. 102.
[60] Wendt, *Teaching,* p. 192 and Stevens, *Teaching,* p. 73.
[61] *Ibid.*

kingdom and trust the Father to care for the necessities of life (Matt. 6:25-33).

When the child of God turns to service, he is sure of a divine helper. It is the Father who is "Lord of the harvest" and who sends forth laborers into his harvest (Matt. 9:38; Luke 10:2). Service may involve one in persecution. If it does he can rely upon the Father to aid him. "For what you are to say will be given you in that hour; for it is not you who speak, but the Spirit of your Father speaking through you" (Matt. 10:18-20). Thus, the child of God may go to his task knowing that his ministry will be sustained by the power and presence of his heavenly Father.

One privilege of childhood is to know that one is loved, that the concerns of one's life are the concerns of his father. Many earthly fathers fail to meet this need. Not so with our heavenly Father! We may be sure of his constant concern. We may rely on his help. We may be continually sustained by his presence. This is our birthright if we are sons of God.

Second, fatherhood of God means that he answers the prayers of his children. Here, as in so many other places, Jesus taught primarily by his practice. The Gospel writers, especially Luke, are careful to record a number of occasions when he prayed. He prayed at his baptism (Luke 3:21), at the feeding of the five thousand (Mark 6:41), at the feeding of the four thousand (Mark 8:6-7), before challenging the faith of the disciples at Caesarea-Philippi (Luke 9:18), at the transfiguration (Luke 9:28-29), before giving the Lord's Prayer (Luke 11:1), when he blessed the little children (Mark 10:13-16), at the institution of the Lord's supper (Luke 22:17-19), and when he broke bread with the two disciples at Emmaus (Luke 24:30-31). It seems that his prayer was what opened their eyes so that they recognized him. Could it be that his praying reminded them of his habit during his life?

Other passages tell us of the habit of prayer that characterized the religious devotion of Jesus. After healing Peter's mother-in-law and the multitudes on the sabbath, "in the morning, a great while before day, he rose and went out to a lonely place, and there he prayed" (Mark 1:35). During his active, Galilean ministry, Jesus "continued his practice of retiring to lonely places and praying" (Luke 5:16, my translation). Before he chose the twelve, he spent the night in prayer (Luke 6:12-13). He assured Peter that he had prayed for him (Luke 22:31-32).[62]

A study of the prayer life of Jesus reveals four principles of prayer as it relates to the fatherhood of God. (1) Prayer, for the son of God, should not be an occasional call from the depths of despair and need; it should be a constant and continuing fellowship with God in all the ways of life. The Father does listen to the cry of despair; but he is more pleased when prayer is practiced as a way of life. (2) Prayer, for Jesus, was a way of expressing his constant dependence on the guidance of the Father. In every great event and turning point in his ministry, prayer played a vital part. He not only talked to God: he also listened to him. Prayer ought to be a two-way intercourse in which we speak to God about our problems but also permit God to speak to us about our lives. (3) Jesus exemplified in his prayer life the quality of absolute self-committal to the Father. His prayer was never selfish because he was never selfish. He looked on prayer, not as a way to get the Father to do his will, but as a way by which he might do the Father's will. (4) His prayer life shows an unwavering confidence in the Father's love, power, and wisdom. He sought God's will because he knew that what God wills is our benefit. He sought God's guidance because he believed that God's choice is always the best choice. He sought God's help because he believed that no problem was beyond his ability to help.

Jesus not only prayed to the Father himself; he also taught his disciples to pray in the *same* way with the *same* attitudes and with the *same* expectations. He taught them that God was their Father and that he delighted to give them good gifts. He would no more deny the requests of his children than an earthly father would deny such requests. Arguing from the lesser to the greater, he said, "If you then, who are evil, know how to give good gifts to your children, how much more will your father who is in heaven give good things to those who ask him?" (Matt. 7:11). Since this is true, the disciple should make a habit of petitioning the Father with the assurance that God will make a habit of giving in return (Matt. 7:7-8). He assured them that the prayer of faith could move mountains (Mark 11:23-24). The man who prayed could believe that he had already

---

[62] For a fuller discussion of Jesus' practice of prayer and the Lord's Prayer, see my book, *Prayer in the New Testament* (Philadelphia: Westminster, 1966), pp. 27-57.

received the answer to his request. He assured them that God was always ready to answer quickly. He is not like the friend who had to be begged before he would render the help he should have rendered simply because he was a friend (Luke 11:5-8). Nor is he like the judge who had to be heckled by the widow before he would do what he should have done without being asked (Luke 18:1-8). Consequently, the disciple should "always . . . pray" and "not lose heart" (Luke 18:1).

But his teaching on prayer found its climax in what we call the Lord's Prayer (Matt. 6:9-13; Luke 11:2-4). Manson has called this prayer "the sum of the teaching of Jesus on the Fatherhood of God." It teaches that everything that concerns a child of God "from his highest ideals to his humblest needs" is the concern of the Father also.[63] Luke gives a shorter account of the prayer; Matthew expands it. Even if we look on the expansion as coming from Matthew and his church, the prayer is essentially the same in both accounts. Some have said that the prayer, especially the first part, is a prayer for God to act without any attendant action on man's part. I doubt that. I would be inclined to agree with those who look upon all the petitions of the prayer as asking for God to make our action effective. Others have insisted that the prayer was meant for the messianic age, that it has no relevance to the everyday needs of our present life. I would deny that. Each individual petition represents a daily need of the disciple in Jesus' day and of the Christian in our day.

It has often been noticed and rightly that the prayer is divided into two parts. The first part is concerned with the things that affect God's rule in the hearts of his children and in the world—"Hallowed be thy name;" "thy kingdom come;" "thy will be done." The child of God must be concerned primarily with God's rule. Otherwise, he cannot expect his heavenly Father to be concerned about his needs. But the second part deals with our personal concerns—"Give us our daily bread;" "Forgive us our sins;" "Deliver us from temptation." Such petitions, Jesus would insist, are proper. God is concerned about our bread, our sins, and our temptations. He is anxious to be enlisted to enable us to live victorious lives in the world.

The Model Prayer was meant to become a pattern of prayer; it was given, not to be repeated, but to be prayed. Many principles of prayer are revealed in it. (1) Prayer should be brief; no holy

[63] *Teaching*, p. 115.

loquacity is needed when dealing with the Father. He does not need to be persuaded to answer; thus the piling up of many words is "empty babbling" after the manner of pagans (Matt. 6:7). He does not need to be informed about our needs; he already knows about them (Matt. 6:8). Because he is the loving Father, he needs only to be given the opportunity to help us. This is what prayer does. (2) Prayer should be simple. This prayer with sharp, arrowlike swiftness drives to the heart of the child's need. (3) Prayer should deal with basic needs of life. This prayer presents needs which are common to all men; it speaks of the deepest level of man's existence under the rule of God. (4) Prayer must flow out from an attitude of self-commitment to the will and purpose of God in the world. Prayer is not a way to control God; it is a way to let God control us. (5) Prayer must be childlike. This prayer breathes of a childlike trust in the Father's providence. One who prays without trusting both himself and his problem to the Father is not likely to be answered.

By his own practice and by his teaching, Jesus taught that the Father answers prayer. Here, in summary, is his entire thought about God. True, the Old Testament and Judaism made much of prayer. But the teaching of Jesus speaks of prayer in such intimate and personal terms that it becomes entirely new. The God who answers prayer is seen in an entirely new light.

We have seen how Jesus took up and refined the Old Testament conception of God and made it Christian. Many Old Testament conceptions were accepted without material change; others were changed considerably; some were transformed entirely. In his teaching lies the basis of Christian thought about God. In him and his teaching we see God as he really is.

CHAPTER VIII
THE MEANING OF DISCIPLESHIP

Jesus had disciples; in this respect he was like other Jewish rabbis. One of his first public acts was to call Peter, Andrew, James, and John (Mark 1:16-20). They left their nets, their vocation, and their family to follow him. These four became the nucleus of a number of disciples who followed Jesus throughout his ministry.

In some important respects, however, Jesus was different from other Jewish rabbis. He called his disciples while the Jewish rabbis seemed to have accepted any who sought to learn from them. Jesus always took the initiative; at least this is true in the cases where the matter is mentioned in the tradition.[1] Jesus' disciples followed *him;* Jewish disciples learned from their masters. The verb "to learn" is found only three times in the Gospels; only once is it used with reference to an attitude to be learned from Jesus (Matt. 11:28). The other two usages are found in Matthew 9:13 and Mark 13:28 which is parallel to Matthew 24:32. Jewish disciples were primarily learners; Jesus'

[1] K. H. Rengstorf, *TDNT*, V. 4, pp. 444-445.

disciples submitted to his authority and were loyal to his person. Jewish disciples hoped to become rabbis themselves; Jesus' disciples were not to expect this (Matt. 23:8). Their destiny was simply to be disciples. Discipleship was not an intermediate step with them, a means to an end; it was an end in itself.

In discussing the meaning of discipleship in the teaching of Jesus, three common errors must be avoided. *First,* we must not confuse what it meant to be a disciple of Jesus and what it means to live a Christian life. Discipleship is a good word to describe the relation of Jesus and his followers during his earthly life; it is not a good word to describe the relation of Jesus to his adherents after the resurrection. The use of the word, disciple, in the New Testament shows this to be true. It is found a total of two hundred and sixty-two times in the New Testament (in Matthew seventy-three; in Mark forty-six; in Luke thirty-seven; in John seventy-eight; in Acts twenty-eight). It is striking that the word is not found at all in the Epistles and that its use definitely diminishes in Acts. Before the resurrection, Jesus' followers were disciples; after the resurrection, they were believers, the elect, the saints, or Christians (to use a modern term seldom found in the New Testament). During his lifetime, they followed him; after his resurrection, they worshiped him. It is true that the principles of discipleship and Christian living are closely related, but they are not the same. The center of gravity shifts from obedience to God to commitment to Christ after the resurrection. The principles of Christian living, developed in the Christian churches, were no doubt based on the teaching of Jesus about meaning of discipleship, but there is a subtle difference which must be maintained.

Second, we must avoid thinking of Jesus as a teacher of universal ethics. His teachings were not directed to all men; they were directed to his disciples. A prior commitment to God is always presupposed. The call of Jesus to his opponents and to the crowds was, "repent." Any demand that went beyond that presupposed repentance and forgiveness as a necessary preparation for obedience. Thus, the Sermon on the Mount is a description of the kingdom man, i.e., the man who has already entered the kingdom of God. This was certainly the thought of Luke who records that the Sermon was addressed only to the disciples (Luke 6:20). Of course, the teachings of Jesus may be used to point the way toward a system of ethics; but it is not that. In the sense of an ethical theory applicable to all men, we would agree with Bultmann that "Jesus teaches no ethics at all." [2]

Third, we must avoid the danger of turning the demands of Jesus into rules to be followed. Jesus always spoke concretely, but there was no attempt to create a new code of laws. He condemned legalism of all kinds as we shall see. His demands were made in the light of definite situations. He expected men to make decisions, but he did not expect the situation to reveal the right choice. He recognized that the disciple needed guidance in applying his commitment to God in the various situations of life. Thus, his demands were more in the nature of illustrations than rules. They may be helpful guides to us in making our decisions, but only if we use them as guidelines rather than as legalistic regulations.

1. Obedience to God Is the Primary Demand of Discipleship

Jesus shared the view of the contemporary Jew that obedience to God was man's duty. God confronted each man with definite demands which he must obey or disobey. His destiny depended on his choice.[3]

(1) Jesus interpreted the idea of obedience radically. This was the primary difference between Jesus and the Jews.[4] Obedience meant total commitment without qualification or reserve. No area of life is immune; obedience is required in everything.[5] No halfhearted obedience is acceptable; God does not claim something from us; he claims *us.*[6] The whole man, not specific acts from man, is what is required.[7] When Zacchaeus promised to restore fourfold to those he had cheated and to give half of his fortune to the poor, Jesus saw in that promise the proof of forgiveness. He exclaimed: "Today salvation has come to this house" (Luke 19:9).

a. *Jesus is himself the preeminent illustration* of what radical obedience means. He never held himself up as an example, but his fidelity to the will of God up to and including the cross is an illustration of the kind of obedience demanded of disciples. When Satan tempted him to forsake the way of suffering which God had revealed was his, Jesus resisted and overcame him (Matt. 4:1-11; Luke 4:1-13). When Peter tried to persuade him that he would not die, Jesus de-

[2] *Jesus,* p. 84.
[3] Kümmel, *Theologie,* p. 42.
[4] Bultmann, *Jesus,* p. 73.
[5] Fuller, *Acts of God,* p. 270.
[6] Conzelmann, *Outline,* p. 118.
[7] Bultmann, *Jesus,* p. 92.

nounced him as speaking with the voice of Satan (Mark 8:31-32). Total commitment to the Father's will led him to pray, "Yet not what I will, but what thou wilt" when he faced the cross (Mark 14:36). Always and in everything his aim was to do God's will. Someone has truly said that if we urged people to pray as Jesus prayed, they would think we were fanatics. His love for men, his devotion to God, his constant concern to help all stand as a shining example of what it means to obey God radically.

b. *Jesus made radical demands* which involved total commitment to God. The first and greatest command is: "You shall love the Lord your God with all your heart, and with all your soul, and with all your mind, and with all your strength" (Mark 12:29-30). Devotion to God must be utterly exclusive; no one nor nothing can share it. "You cannot serve God and mammon" (Matt. 6:24). Jesus felt that it was proper to render unto Caesar what belonged to Caesar, but he did not miss the opportunity to remind them that they must also render unto "God the things that are God's" (Mark 12:17). The "meek" are those who voluntarily submit themselves to God. Jesus said they alone would find the true meaning of earthly life; they would inherit the earth (Matt. 5:5). Commitment to God should change man's whole set of values. No longer should he seek to lay up earthly treasure; his concern should now be with heavenly treasure (Matt. 6:19-21). The least in the kingdom of heaven is he who takes lightly the least of the commandments and teaches others to do so. The greatest is he who both keeps and teaches the commandments (Matt. 5:19). The climactic demand of Jesus is: "You, therefore, must be perfect as your heavenly Father is perfect"(Matt. 5:48). Perfect, to the Semitic mind, is that which is completely sound or whole. As applied to men, it means to be true. Jesus' demand meant that the disciple must be whole and undivided in his devotion to God.[8] There is no room for compromise, no divided devotion, in true discipleship.

c. *Jesus felt that inner attitudes* as well as outer actions were important in our obedience to God. The disciple must not only avoid murder; he must forego the burst of wrath and the insulting remark as well (Matt. 5:21-22). Adultery is certainly to be avoided, but so also is the lustful look and thought that leads to adultery (Matt. 5:27-28). The disciple must not swear falsely, but he must also be absolutely honest (Matt. 5:33-37). He must not only forego retaliation against

[8] *Ibid.,* p. 120.

one who wrongs him; he must also refuse to resist evil that men seek to inflict on him (Matt. 5:38-42). He must not only love his friends; he must also love and pray for his enemies (Matt. 5:43-48). These antitheses of the Sermon can be summarized in the words: "Not only . . . but even." [9] The fundamental meaning is that the will of God must be done *completely;* mere outward obedience is no obedience at all.[10]

d. *The disciple must be willing to forsake his family* and follow Jesus. To the Jew, this was perhaps the most radical demand possible; family obligations were paramount with him. Yet Jesus insisted that they must become subordinate to the demands of discipleship. When three men sought to be his disciples but insisted on fulfilling worldly obligations first, Jesus said: "No one who puts his hand to the plow and looks back is fit for the kingdom of God" (Luke 9:62). He also said: "If any one come to me and does not hate his own father and mother and wife and children and brothers and sisters, yes, and even his own life, he cannot be my disciple" (Luke 14:26). Jesus ignored his mother and brothers and claimed his true kin were those who did the will of God (Mark 3:31-35). He demanded that the disciple must do the same. He must renounce even his own life and lose it for the sake of Jesus (Mark 8:35).

e. In a series of sayings *on the word and will of God,* Jesus emphasized that obedience must be radical. More blessed than being Jesus' own mother is the continual hearing and performance of the word of God (Luke 11:28). Mere profession of discipleship gains no one entrance into the kingdom; only those who do the "will of my Father" will enter in (Matt. 7:21-23). The man who hears and does the words of Jesus is like a wise man who builds his house on solid rock (Matt. 7:24).

f. *The disciple's fidelity to God must be unwavering.* He will face persecution; he will even be "hated by all for my name's sake. But he who endures (i.e., stands fast) to the end will be saved" (Mark 13:13). He should consider himself blessed when he is persecuted for righteousness' sake (Matt. 5:10-12). Not that mere physical suffering is spiritually significant; it is not. Rather, persecution speaks of fidelity to God, an unwavering allegiance to his will. This is the basis for rejoicing. The disciple must be alert and on guard against the

[9] Bornkamm, *Jesus,* p. 103.
[10] Bultmann, *Jesus,* pp. 90-91.

snares of Satan. Otherwise, his heart may be "weighed down with dissipation and drunkenness and cares of this life, and that day" come upon him "like a snare" (Luke 21:34). He is to "watch and pray" lest he be overcome by temptation. His spirit may be strong; his flesh, however, is weak (Mark 14:38.) The disciple is to be like a man waiting for his master to return home from the marriage feast; he will want to open *at once* to his knock (Luke 12:35-36). Constant watchfulness and faithfulness is the price he must pay to be ready for the coming of the Son of man (Mark 13:33; Luke 12:40; Matt. 24:42).

g. Jesus demanded that the disciple *obey God without thought of reward*. This shows how radical his demand was. In the parable of the slave who had done everything required of him but does not expect thanks from his master (Luke 17:7-9), Jesus found the teaching, "So you also, when you have done all that is commanded you, say, 'We are unworthy servants; we have only done what was our duty' " (Luke 17:10). The parable of the gracious owner of the vineyard who paid all of his workers equal wages in spite of unequal labor teaches that the disciple can make no claims on God (Matt. 20:1-15).[11] No one can expect to receive a special reward for a special work.[12] The only thing that Jesus could promise James and John when they sought the chief places in the coming kingdom was a share in his cup and baptism, i.e. his sufferings (Mark 10:35-40). So frequently did Jesus teach that discipleship does not mean reward that this must be called a characteristic of his teaching.

On the other hand, there is another strand of teaching, equally characteristic of Jesus, that seems to promise reward for faithful service. Peter is promised that those who forsake all and follow Jesus will receive all that they have forsaken "a hundredfold now in this time" and "in the age to come eternal life" (Mark 10:30). Those who do alms, pray, and fast in secret will be found out and repaid by the Father "who sees in secret" (Matt. 6:4,6,18). Those who seek the kingdom first will have the necessities of life added to them (Matt. 6:33). He who is willing to lose his life for the sake of Jesus is promised that he will "save it" (Mark 8:35 and parallels).

How then can we say that God demands obedience without thought of reward? Bultmann would paradoxically say that God rewards those

[11] *Ibid.,* p. 79.
[12] Kümmel, *Theologie,* p. 50.

who serve without thought of reward.[13] Perhaps three things can be said to reconcile these seemingly contradictory strands in the teaching of Jesus.

First, it is important to notice that there is no thought of an accounting system in which man lays up merit and claims payment from God.[14] The disciple does not earn a *wage;* he is a slave of God and has no claim to payment.[15] There is no thought of repayment for service rendered or a system of meritorious works.

Second, it is important to notice that there is no thought of material rewards for spiritual service. All of the rewards are in terms of heavenly, spiritual realities. This is true even of the houses and lands which Peter was promised a "hundredfold" because he had forsaken all and followed Jesus (Mark 10:30). Ultimately the reward is simply God and fellowship with him.[16]

Third, the reward is not so much "payment in kind" as it is the natural result of the attitudes and actions demanded. The one who is meek will inherit the earth, not as payment for his meekness, but because meekness is the attitude that claims the earth for its heritage (Matt. 5:5). The one who loses his life for Jesus' sake will find the true meaning of life; this is the natural outcome of full surrender.

On the one hand, then, Jesus meant to show that serving with an eye on the reward destroys the very nature of discipleship. Such service would turn discipleship into a secular, worldly, sinful attempt to put God under obligation to us. Such obedience is no obedience at all. On the other hand, Jesus wanted his disciples to know that a life of full surrender to God is not self-defeating. Human personality is not destroyed by obedience; rather, obedience to God is the sure road to human fulfilment. The kind of life which God demands of us is ultimately for our good.

(2) Jesus condemned legalism. What has been said about radical obedience is the reverse side of another strand in Jesus' teaching—his condemnation of legalism. Bultmann sees Jesus' interpretation of the will of God as a great "protest against Jewish legalism." [17] There is no doubt that this is true. In the sabbath controversies, Jesus reminded the people that God had made the sabbath for man "not man for

[13] *Theology,* V. 1, p. 14 and *Jesus,* p. 79; cf. also Reumann, *Jesus,* p. 248.
[14] Kümmel, *Theologie,* pp. 50-51.
[15] Reumann, *Jesus,* p. 248.
[16] *Ibid.*
[17] *Theology,* V. 1, p. 11.

the sabbath" (Mark 2:23 to 3:6, esp 2:27). He repeatedly warned the disciples against the leaven of the Pharisees, a figure of speech for the hypocritical legalism (Mark 8:15; Luke 12:1). Jesus looked upon the current legalistic interpretation of the will of God as a distortion of the law. He condemned it and stood over against it in his teaching. If we examine his teachings carefully, we can find several contrasts between the legalism of the Jews and the demands of Jesus.

a. *Legalism permits self-detachment; Jesus demands total involvement.* Legalism is obedience to the letter of the law. A man may tender that kind of obedience without being involved with God at the deeper level of his existence. The characteristic thing in Judaism was that obedience to God was purely formal.[18] Traditional interpretation of the law had produced a network of regulations behind which a man could hide himself from God.[19]

Jesus set himself against this idea of formal, legalistic obedience. He saw every act as involving the whole man and expressing his inner self. "Every half-way" was an abomination to him.[20] He accused the Pharisees of honoring God with their lips while their heart was far from him (Mark 7:6-8). He warned against false prophets dressed in sheep's clothing. He insisted that good fruit can only come from a good tree, that grapes cannot come from a bramble bush nor thorns from a fig tree. He concluded: "The good man out of the good treasure of his heart produces good, and the evil man out of his evil treasure produces evil; for out of the abundance of the heart his mouth speaks" (Luke 6:45). He likened the disciples to salt and emphasized the necessity of salt retaining its character as salt if it was to be of use to man (Luke 14:34-35; Mark 9:50; Matt. 5:13). In all of this, he was stressing the fact that the whole man is involved in his obedience to God. Actions come forth from character; therefore, character is of primary importance.

b. *Legalism breeds self-righteousness; Jesus demanded absolute sincerity.* If obedience is to a code of rules, it is possible for a man to say, "I have obeyed completely." When the young ruler said to Jesus, "Teacher, all these I have observed from my youth" (Mark 10:20), he was not lying. He had obeyed them in the legalistic way which was common to the Jews. Under legalism self-righteousness

[18] Bultmann, *Theology,* V. 1, pp. 11-12.
[19] Bornkamm, *Jesus,* p. 105.
[20] Bultmann, *Jesus,* p. 93.

is inevitable. It was a curse to the Jews in Jesus' day. Even their religious acts—almsgiving, prayer, and fasting—were directed to impressing men with their piety (Matt. 6:1-18). They loved the chief seats in the synagogue, salutations in the marketplace, and to be addressed by the title "rabbi" (Matt. 23:6-7). They did their deeds to be seen by men, and made "their phylacteries broad and their fringes long" to advertise their superior piety (Matt. 23:5).

Jesus warned his disciples against self-righteousness. He demanded absolute sincerity from them in their religious practices (Matt. 6:1). He recognized the very real temptation for ostentatious display and so he advised them to do their almsgiving, prayer, and fasting in secret (Matt. 6:3,6,17-18). They were not to display their devotion to God before men; they were not to boast of obedience as a human achievement. By his demand for radical obedience, Jesus ruled out the possibility of self-righteousness. When obedience to God *in all things* is taken seriously, religious pride is impossible.

c. *Legalism fosters outer obedience; Jesus demanded inner obedience as well.* One example of the external quality of Jewish obedience is found in Mark 7:3-4. "For the Pharisees, and all the Jews, do not eat unless they wash their hands, observing the tradition of the elders; and when they come from the market place, they do not eat unless they purify themselves; and there are many other traditions which they observe, the washing of cups and pots and vessels of bronze." Mark was here explaining the background of one of the most important teachings of Jesus to his Gentile readers.

When the Pharisees, in the light of these customs, challenged the piety of the disciples because they did not wash their hands before eating, Jesus replied: "There is nothing outside a man which by going into him can defile him; but the things which come out of a man are what defile him" (Mark 7:15). When the disciples were puzzled by this saying, he pointed out that what a man eats is digested and eliminated. Thus, it cannot defile a man. But what a man speaks, he speaks from the heart. This is where defilement really is, in the man himself. His spirituality cannot be judged by his failure to obey minute food regulations (Mark 7:18-23). The difference between Jesus and current Judaism is that Jesus demanded the whole man for God. Obedience must touch man at the deepest level of life; he cannot obey without *being* obedient.

d. *Legalism promotes casuistry; Jesus demanded unreserved obedience.*

When a man is confronted with regulations, he seeks holes in the law. He wants to claim to have obeyed without actually having done so. The technical name for this practice is casuistry. Jewish lawyers were adept at it. Jesus accused them of loading men with heavy burdens while refusing to touch them with their own fingers (Luke 11:46). They knew where to find the escape hatches in the law.

One example of this is found in Matthew 23:16-22. Oaths, it was said, on certain things, such as the Temple or the altar, were not binding. If a man swore by these, he need not perform his oath. But oaths on other things, such as the gold in the Temple or the sacrifices on the altar, were binding. If a man swore by these, he must perform his oath. If you were on the "inside" you could swear without obligation. Such regulations were meant to catch the unwary and open the way for dishonesty by greedy men.

Another example of casuistry is found in Mark 7:9-13. The law which said that a man must honor his father and mother, meant, among other things, that he must support them with his material possessions if they needed it. The Jews had a regulation which permitted a man to dedicate his possessions to God without actually releasing control of them. Thus, he could say to his parents, "What you would have gained from me is Corban (that is, given to God) (v. 12). Jesus said, concerning this custom, "You have a fine way of rejecting the commandment of God" (v. 9), you make "void the word of God through your tradition which you hand on. And many such things you do" (v. 13).

Jesus completely condemned such practices; he would have nothing to do with them.[21] He was unique in his absolute, unconditional demands which swept away all reserve or compromise.[22]

e. *Legalism makes all laws equal; Jesus distinguished between the greater and the lesser.* The battle cry of the legalist is, "sin is sin, black is black, white is white." He regards all laws as equally binding and equally important. This enables him to concentrate on doing the small things that cost him little and neglect the greater things that demand sacrifice. Jesus condemned this in the Pharisee who prided himself on tithing mint, rue, and every herb while neglecting weightier matters such as justice, mercy, faith, and love of God (Matt. 23:23; Luke 11:42). He did not condemn their tithing; he condemned

[21] Bornkamm, *Jesus,* p. 105.
[22] H. K. McArthur, *Understanding the Sermon on the Mount* (London: Epworth Press, 1960), p. 54.

their neglect of greater matters. "These you ought to have done," he said, "without neglecting the others." Perhaps the hypocrites who devoured widows' houses and made long prayers for a pretense (Mark 12:40; Luke 20:47) were subject to the same error.

Jesus, on the other hand, discriminated between lesser and greater commandments. The greatest was to love God completely; the second was to love neighbor as self (Mark 12:29-32). This much lies on the surface of his teaching. Much more lies below the surface. He eliminated the nonessential and concentrated on the essential.[23] Jews have often claimed that all of Jesus' teachings can be paralleled in their Talmud. To some degree, this is true. But when one reads the Talmud, he must search diligently and long for the parallels. They are so intertwined with senseless and superficial regulations that the nature of the Talmud as a spiritual guide is completely different from the teaching of Jesus.

f. *Legalism leaves room for works of supererogation; Jesus demanded total obedience.* When ethical demands are reduced to specific statutes, many cases are left uncovered. No amount of legislation can cover every imaginable situation. Thus, the way is opened for all kinds of sinful desire and passion which are not prohibited. Moreover, the way is open to consider acts which are not demanded as works that go beyond obedience, i.e. works of supererogation. The legalist can claim extra merit for extra works. The Pharisee, as he prayed in the Temple, boasted, "I fast twice a week, I give tithes of all that I get" (Luke 18:12). Private fasting was not required by the law; tithes were demanded from agricultural products only.[24] Thus, the Pharisee was claiming extra merit for works that went beyond demands of the law.

Jesus refused to recognize this as true. He said that the Pharisee was not accepted in the eyes of God (Luke 18:14). Further, he taught that the disciple should consider himself to be a slave of God with no claim of wages for work done. When he had done all that was required of him, he was to say, "I am an unworthy servant; I have only done what was my duty" (cf. Luke 17:10). Jesus demanded total obedience.

g. *Legalism reveres the law; Jesus demanded commitment to God.* It is the nature of legalism to substitute the law for God, to forget

---

[23] *Ibid*, p. 53.
[24] S. M. Gilmour, "Luke," *Interpreter's Bible*, V. 8, p. 309.

that God is the authority behind the law. This is true in modern bibliolatry as it was in ancient legalism. The act of obedience, as well as the thing obeyed, tends to be separated from God and become man's real authority.[25] Jesus waged unceasing war against obedience which was not directed toward God. It was God who was man's authority; it was God who must be obeyed. The law might express, however inadequately, his will; it must not be substituted for him.

h. *Legalism stresses the negative; Jesus stressed the positive.* The law usually speaks in terms of "thou shalt not." Jewish regulations were overwhelming negative in nature. Many modern Christians measure their piety in terms of what they do not do. This is contrary to the teaching of Jesus. The disciple was to do "good works" (Matt. 5:16). He was to show mercy (Matt. 5:7). He was to give to him who asked him (Luke 6:30). He was to seek the kingdom (Matt. 6:33). The accent is on the positive qualities and actions of life just as it was with Jesus himself. Prohibitions do exist for the disciple, but his true self is measured by what he does, not by what he does not do.

(3) Jesus did not, however, abolish the law or law itself. What has been said about legalism should not be taken to mean that Jesus abolished the Law of Moses or that he denied the usefulness of spiritual laws. The starting place in his exposition of the will of God was the Old Testament.[26] He asserted that he had not come to "abolish the law and the prophets" but that he had come to "fulfil them" (Matt. 5:17). McArthur insists that Jesus' teaching was a legitimate development of the Mosaic tradition. For proof, he appeals to three things. (1) Jesus was a devout Jew who appealed to the Old Testament for support. (2) Many scholars have been able to maintain that there is no contradiction between the Sermon on the Mount and the Pentateuch. (3) Most of the teaching of Jesus can be paralleled from rabbinic literature.[27]

Bornkamm is quick to point out that Jesus is not the prophet of fanatics who would sacrifice the past for the sake of a dreamed-for future. His respect for the law is shown by his sending the leper to offer the sacrifices of thanksgiving for his healing that the law demanded (Mark 1:44), by his command that the scribes were to be obeyed since they sit on Moses throne (Matt. 23:2), and by the

---

[25] Bornkamm, *Jesus,* p. 104.
[26] Conzelmann, *Outline,* p. 116.
[27] *Understanding,* p. 48.

fact that he was guest in the house of Pharisees on more than one occasion (Luke 8:36; 9:37; 14:1).[28] Jesus certainly did not approve of fanatical disregard for the law. He would have agreed with Paul: "The Law is holy, and the commandment is holy and just and good" (Rom. 7:12). He would not have agreed with modern scholars who see any kind of law or ethical regulation as contrary to the concept of radical obedience to God.

Bultmann comes dangerously close to this in his discussion of human decisions.[29] He seems to be saying that God trusts man to make the right decision for himself, that all the guidance man would need would be found in the situation that calls for decision. He seems to leave no place for the Bible as a guide to proper decision nor for the work of the Holy Spirit in leading men. To me, this is an overly radical statement of the meaning of radical obedience.

Jesus did give his disciples definite instructions. This does not mean that he was the giver of a better law than that of Moses. It is impossible to regard the teaching of Jesus as an attempt to define all human behavior. But he did recognize the need for guidance beyond that which man can see for himself in a particular situation. His own teaching was in the form of concrete illustrations of what the will of God demanded in certain situations.[30] I think it would be valid to view the law of Moses in the same way.

What Jesus protested against was regarding the law rather than God as the ultimate authority for life. He condemned those who viewed the law as defining the whole duty of man. He would have protested Christian use of his own teaching in this way. But he recognized that we need guidance. Otherwise it will be impossible for us to judge what the will of God is in the situations of our own life. We may, it may be said, depend on the Holy Spirit to guide us. This is true, but it is not always easy to distinguish the leadership of the Holy Spirit from our own natural and sinful inclinations. Self-deception is the easiest kind of deception. Thus, we have cases of men claiming that the Holy Spirit has led them to break up homes, commit adultery, murder men, and deceive others.

This would be impossible if we took the law of Moses and the teachings of Jesus seriously as indicating *the kind* of responses which

---

[28] Bornkamm, *Jesus*, pp. 101-102.
[29] *Jesus*, p. 83.
[30] Fuller, *Acts of God*, p. 270.

obedience requires. One may be more adequate than the other, but both are useful. We may never have the opportunity of literally "turning the other cheek." We will often have the opportunity and obligation of making responses of *the same kind.* We see then that Jesus did not mean to destroy the Law. He fulfilled it by his own life and teaching and left it to be a guide for his disciples.

2. Love Is the Central Demand in Human Relationships

At first glance, it is surprising that Jesus uses the word, love, so rarely.[31] There are only three connections in which Jesus used the word to express the meaning of discipleship. (1) There is the command to love God with the whole being; Jesus called this the greatest commandment (Mark 12:29-30 and parallels). (2) There is the command to love our neighbor as ourselves; Jesus called this the second commandment which is of the same nature as the first (Mark 10:31 and parallels). (3) There is the command to love one's enemies (Matt. 5:44; Luke 6:27,35).

Nor were these commandments to love original with Jesus. With the exception of the command to love our enemies, they are found in the Old Testament. Even pagan religions contain admonitions to love our fellowmen.[32] But this does not mean that the command of love is not unique and central in the teaching of Jesus.

It is unique with him in its basis. With Jesus, love for others is not based on the worth of the person loved or the character of the one loving; it is based on obedience to God (Matt. 5:48; Luke 6:36). In pagan religions, love for others was based on the worth of humanity.[33] In Southern culture in America, love for others was based on the character of the one loving; one loved others because he was too much of a gentleman not to. Not so with Jesus. He taught us to love because it was godlike, because it was demanded by our relation to God. Love was obedience (cf. John 14:21).

Jesus' command to love was also unique in its nature. Love is not thought of as an emotion, a feeling of goodwill, or respect for others. It is thought of as an attitude of the will, a matter of deliberate choice.[34] It is a principle of concern for the good of others which is willing to sacrifice to achieve that good. This is preeminently illustrated in

[31] Bultmann, *Jesus,* p. 110.
[32] *Ibid.,* p. 111.
[33] *Ibid.*
[34] *Ibid.,* p. 117.

the parable of the good Samaritan (Luke 10:29-37). Jesus used the parable to answer the question, "Who is my neighbor?" He told of a Samaritan (a detested and detestable person to the Jew) who gave unselfish help to a Jew who had been ignored by his own religious countrymen. He endangered his own life by going to the assistance of the other; he walked while the wounded man rode on his animal; he paid for his continued care in the inn. In all of this he was demonstrating an unselfish concern for another man, one who under other circumstances would have been his enemy, at considerable sacrifice to himself. This is what love meant to Jesus. This is how one obeyed God and acted like him.

That love was central in the teaching of Jesus is seen in the number of times that Jesus taught this principle without using the word. The apparent paucity of love passages is an illusion. Often the *thing itself* is demanded when the word is not used. For instance in the Lukan passage: "Love your enemies, do good to those who hate you, bless those who curse you, pray for those who abuse you" (Luke 6:27-28), "doing good," "blessing," and "praying for" are looked upon as love in action. One who does these things for his enemies loves them.

Many other passages have the same emphasis. If one loves, he will not make a habit of criticizing. He will not seek to correct his brother's faults until he has corrected his own (Matt. 7:1-5). If one loves, he will seek to do unto others as he would that others would do unto him (Matt. 7:12). This means that he will take the trouble to understand the situation of the other; he will seek the solution to the other's problems which he would want applied to his own if he were in the same situation; he will then *act* in behalf of the other. The so-called Golden Rule is no easy thing; it demands real sympathy and understanding as well as readiness to sacrifice. It is love in action. Again, if one loves others he will see to it that his life, actions, and words do not constitute a reason for their sinning. He will not lead "the little ones" into sin (Mark 9:42-48 and parallels).

Forgiveness is but another word for love and the command to forgive is frequent in the teaching of Jesus. "If your brother sins, rebuke him, and if he repents, forgive him" (Luke 17:3). "How often?" asked Peter, "seven times?" Jesus replied, "I do not say to you seven times, but seventy times seven" (Matt. 18:22). One who prays for forgiveness must also be willing to forgive (Mark 11:25; Matt. 6:14-15). One who offers a gift to God must first go and be reconciled to his brother if he wants his gift accepted (Matt. 5:23-24). The parable of the unforgiving steward teaches that forgiveness is a primary requirement of discipleship (Matt. 18:23-35). Forgiveness is love in action. Perhaps it is the hardest of all commands to obey. Bultmann has pointed out that one can force himself to do good to others, to pray for him, but forgiveness is only possible if one really loves.[35]

Love itself lies at the heart of the commands of Jesus to forego retaliation, to turn the other cheek, to go the second mile, to give to the one asking without expecting repayment (Matt. 5:38-42; Luke 6:29-30). The reinterpretation of the law of murder to forbid anger and scorn is a demand for love; why is one angry with another if he does not look on the other man as servant to his own desires? The interpetation of the law of adultery to forbid lust is but another way of saying that one must not look on another as a means to an end, but an end in themselves. The reinterpretation of the law of oaths to forbid dishonesty is but another way of saying that one must love others (Matt. 5:21-37 and parallels).

There can be no doubt then that the command to love is central in the teaching of Jesus. It surfaces at almost every point where the relationship of disciples with other men is in question.

Is self-love forbidden by Jesus? Some say that it is. The answer depends on your definition of love. In the sense of self-admiration, self-seeking, or self-righteousness, it is certainly forbidden. But in the sense of seeking our highest good, it is commanded. Love for self is the standard by which we judge whether or not we love others. Only as we seek their highest good to the same degree that we seek our own can we say that we love them. Only when we care for them to the same extent that we care for ourselves can we really love them. Thus self-love is demanded of the disciple. Otherwise, the command to love our neighbor as ourself would be nonsense.

3. Discipleship Meant Mission

We should not expect to find a fully developed doctrine of mission in the teaching of Jesus. His central concern was to impart an understanding of God and his kingdom, to lay the foundation for a life of discipleship. Yet, we do find indications in the teaching of Jesus that discipleship involved mission. The early churches were expressing

---

[35] *Ibid.*, pp. 116-117.

a genuine remembrance of Jesus when they insisted that every Christian was a missionary, a witness, and an evangelist.

The connection between discipleship and mission comes to the surface in Jesus' call of his first disciples (Mark 1:16-20). He told them he would make them to become "fishers of men" (Mark 1:17), or as Luke records it, "you will be catching men" (Luke 5:10). At first, the word seems surprising. We use the same kind of language to describe those who "trap" or "hook" others for their own designs. But in the mouth of Jesus, the word does not mean to outwit and use another man; it means to catch him for the kingdom of God.[36]

When he appointed the twelve, a twofold consequence is stated; they were to be "with him" and be "sent out to preach" (Mark 3:14-15). It is actually recorded that he did send them out to preach, two-by-two. First the twelve were sent (Mark 6:7-11 and parallels), and then seventy were sent (Luke 10:1-16). The harvest of the Lord was to be their concern. They were to pray the Lord to send forth laborers into his harvest (Matt. 9:37-38).

The kingdom man is to seek first the kingdom of God (Matt. 6:33) and pray for its coming (Matt. 6:10). Whatever else these commands mean, they mean that the disciple is to be concerned about and involved in the extension of God's rule in the hearts of men. The same conception of task is involved in the metaphors of "salt of the earth" and "light of the world" (Matt. 5:13-16; cf. Mark 4:21; 9:49-50; Luke 8:16; 14:34-35). The disciples were to perform good works in such a way that God would be glorified through their works (Matt. 5:16). They were given the keys of the kingdom (Matt. 16:19) and were to mediate to the world the prior actions of God. (Note the future perfects in this verse which clearly indicate that the prior action is in heaven. The disciples were only to pronounce what heaven had done.) They were to be faithful in their testimony even though it meant that they would be delivered to councils, flogged, and dragged before governors and kings for the sake of Jesus (Matt. 10:17).

When the man out of whom Jesus had cast the legion of demons asked Jesus to accompany him, Jesus replied: "Return to your home, and declare how much God has done for you" (Luke 8:39). The parable of the pounds (Luke 19:11-27) in which the slaves were entrusted with money to trade and get gain for their absentee lord teaches that disciples were to be good stewards of all that they pos-

---

[36] Bornkamm, *Jesus*, pp. 148-149.

sessed. The parable of the wicked husbandmen from whom the vineyard of the lord was wrested and entrusted to others (Mark 12:1-12) teaches faithfulness in performing the tasks God has assigned.

The parables of the lost sheep, the lost coin, and the lost brothers (Luke 15) imply that the disciple should share the concern of God for what is lost and the joy of God in that which is found. The great judgment scene shows that discipleship means feeding the hungry, welcoming the stranger, clothing the naked, and visiting the sick and imprisoned (Matt. 25:34-39). To do this for others is to do it for Jesus. In all of these passages, Jesus was teaching that discipleship involved more than the enjoyment of God's fellowship and blessing. It involved mission, task, stewardship, and concern for the cause of God in the world. The command to mission with which both Matthew and Luke complete their Gospels is meant to show that the call to discipleship was essentially a call to mission (Matt. 28:16-20; Luke 24:47-49).

Among other things, the mission of discipleship involved life within the group. It may be wrong to say that Jesus founded a church. It is not wrong to say that he laid the foundation for the church idea in his training of the disciples. There is never any hint of the individual, isolated disciple. The idea of involvement in group life is essential and inerradicable in the gospel tradition.